"The stories in this book reminded me of songs by Woody Guthrie and art by Marc Chagall: rays of hope lighting up a dark landscape. This is a book to be cherished."
— Eboo Patel, author of *Interfaith Leadership: A Primer*

"Sandhya's stated goal—which she ably achieves here—is simple yet arduous: to get us out of our stifling cynicism so that we may see deeply, listen intently, act justly, and love radically. To break down our world-weariness and its consequent inactivity, she beautifully fuses the enduring wisdom of faith and justice movements with the raw tactility and wounded victories of on-the-ground work, in ways that both disarm and charm. To be sure, her scholarship is needed more than ever, for it is nuanced yet accessible, technical yet gritty, erudite yet disruptive."
— José Francisco Morales Torres, Director of Pastoral Formation, Disciples Seminary Foundation, Claremont, California

"Describing the convicted, creative, courageous initiatives of people in our own communities, Sandhya Jha focuses a narrative beam of light on the moral arc of the universe as it bends toward justice. Thank you, Sandhya, for helping us lift our eyes to see possibility and hope—and a pathway to our own involvement."
— Sharon E. Watkins, author of *Whole: A Call to Unity in Our Fragmented World*

"I can be overwhelmed by the call to live transformative love in the world—to house the homeless, restore souls, repair relationships, generate justice. So I am very grateful for Sandhya Rani Jha's book. She doesn't deal in empty aspirations. Instead, she describes community-change models that are actually working. Jha not only knows what I hope for, she shows me how to get there. I need this good news. I think we all do."
— Andrew Dreitcer, Center for Engaged Compassion at Claremont School of Theology

"Jha pulls no punches in this enlivening report from the front lines of social justice activism and our common life together: 'Protests aren't enough. And experts can't fix communities from the outside.' If you're looking for hope amidst the turmoil of our times alongside practical strategies to enhance your own work, read each chapter and take notes in the margins. From innovative prison programs and new church models like Gordon Cosby's Church of the Saviour, you'll find inspiration."

— Rob Wilson-Black, Chief Executive Officer, Sojourners

"In this practical and inspiring guide, Sandhya Jha teaches us how to lean on the arc of the moral universe so that it bends towards justice. In our exhaustion and desperation, Jha infuses hope into every page."

— Carol Howard Merritt, pastor and author of *Healing Spiritual Wounds*

"My South African friend Episcopal priest Rene August, says that the difference between a marathon and a sprint is how you breathe. Many of us are finding ourselves in a marathon at this historic moment and we need books that make us take a deep breath. *Transforming Communities* is such a book; it draws our attention to the good news happening in communities around us in a way that strengthens our faith—while providing us with practical advice designed to encourage and equip."

— Alexia Salvatierra, coauthor of *Faith-Rooted Organizing: Mobilizing the Church in Service to the World*

"Sandhya Rani Jha has provided a timely resource for community leaders to get a handle on how to live and lead faithfully in an increasingly polarized world savaged and torn apart by racism, sexism, xenophobia, economic disparity, and political isolation. She surveyed our recent history and mined from it gems of community transformation led by the local people for the local people. She did not glamorize these stories but shared them holistically with their successes and struggles that came with challenging the status quo. Along the way, she showed how relational and truth-telling tools such as asset-based community development, restorative justice, World Café, and truth commission are essential for transforming communities in our context today. The "Learn More" section of each chapter is invaluable for further learning and connecting with these tools and resources beyond this book. I know I will refer to this book again and again in my ministry of empowering church leaders to create sustainable communities."

— Eric H. F. Law, Executive Director, Kaleidoscope Institute, and
    author of several books including *Holy Currencies*

"In our transitional, diasporic age, the possibility of true 'community' seems lost in the face of daunting rates of isolation, addiction, and structural violence. Yet Sandhya Jha dares each of us to imagine ourselves as grassroots organizers wholly prepared to challenge and calm the tempest of political winds now blowing nationwide. Complementing an intersectional diagnosis of our manifold social ills with practical examples of effective, justice-centered change, Jha offers an inspiring reminder that we hold immense power to make our communities right again."

— Ethan Vesely-Flad, Director of National Organizing, Fellowship
    of Reconciliation

TRANSFORMING COMMUNITIES

How People Like You Are Healing Their Neighborhoods

Sandhya Rani Jha

chalice
press

Saint Louis, Missouri

An imprint of Christian Board of Publication

Photo of Sandhya Rani Jha by Brooke Anderson
Cover design and art: Jesse Turri

www.ChalicePress.com

Print: 9780827237155   EPUB:9780827237162   EPDF: 9780827237179

Printed in the United States of America

Contents

In the spring of 2014, I met with a colleague as I was finishing up my manuscript for my last book on race and faith in America. He asked how I was doing.

"I wonder if I'm suffering from depression," I said.

"Well, you've been living in the narrative of systemic racism nonstop for the past 6 months," he responded. "I'm not shocked to hear that."

That summer I started a little podcast called "Hope from the Hood," telling stories of the good things the small nonprofits I work with are doing. In fact, I was editing my first episode when the idea for this book emerged, and they were both part of the same reality that finally dawned on me:

> *I can't keep living in the morass of how this nation is failing, I thought. I need to ground myself in stories of hope. I need to delve into the possibilities for a better world if I'm going to help build it.*

This book is dedicated to the people I get to work with on a daily basis at the Oakland Peace Center who remind me not to give up hope. It's dedicated to the people who are actually building what Dr. King called "Beloved Community" brick by brick, garden row by garden row, inmate by inmate, and registered voter by registered voter. We do not look up from our work often enough to realize how much we've done.

Look up. People are paying attention. You're making the world people want to live in. Thank you.

Introduction

"You can't have a cooperative without cooperators."
—JOSE MARIA ARIZMENDIARRIETA

The village of Mondragón[1] was excited to meet its new priest. Until he stepped into the pulpit.

"He spoke in a monotone with intricate and repetitive phraseology difficult to understand. Away with this priest that the Monsignor has imposed upon us, he hardly even reads with any grace! That was the first reaction of the faithful," complained one parishioner.[2] He had really wanted to study sociology in Belgium, and it showed; people found him hard to follow in small group settings as well as during his homilies. They even tried to get "that red priest" (as conservatives in town called him) reassigned, to no avail.

But 25-year-old Father José María Arizmendiarrieta recognized that his small Basque village in the foothills of the Pyrenees was suffering in the wake of the Spanish Civil War. And he knew that the reason they were suffering was lack of opportunity, lack of jobs, and a state government in no way interested or equipped to aid the people they still saw as insurrectionists.

Arizmendi, as he was nicknamed, was a sociologist at heart. After two years of building trust, in 1943 he started youth programs and a soccer league, and he soon launched a training school for villagers to get good jobs. By 1956 his former pupils started a cooperatively owned business making paraffin stoves.

---

1 Mondragón is the Spanish name; it was and sometimes still is known as Arrasate in the local Basque dialect.
2 William Foote Whyte and Kathleen King Whyte, "Making Mondragon: The Growth and Dynamics of the Worker Cooperative Complex," Cornell International Industrial and Labor Relations Reports, 1991, 2

Today, the Mondragon Corporation is the 10th largest business group in Spain with 80,000 employees, many of whom own shares in the company. The region has been transformed, and in a country suffering severe economic strain and massive unemployment, Mondragon Corporation's commitment to caring for its workers as well as providing quality goods ensures the community continues to thrive. And since shares are held by employees, decisions are made by workers.

***

Arizmendi was an ordained Catholic priest, but he was also just a guy—a guy who had watched his region at war with his national government and who had gone to prison for writing about it during his career as a journalist. He wasn't an inspirational preacher. He wasn't even in the job he wanted: sociology. But Arizmendi knew his community was suffering and that the autocratic government wasn't helping poor, jobless people it had deemed resisters. Sermons alone would never lift up the community.

A cooperatively owned corporation *did* lift up the community. And it still does.

***

And that's what this book is about.

The world around us is a wreck. Every newspaper and cable network confirms it for us daily. The lack of connection between neighbors confirms it. The rapid spike in hate crimes confirms it. Many of us are not content with things the way they are; too many people are getting hurt and it is in our nature to feel one another's suffering and be moved by it.

But it can also feel overwhelming. The solutions seem beyond us, like we need a miracle, or at the very least we need a guy with a cape and a bat car to show up.

It could be a long wait.

But I believe there are a million Arizmendis waiting to step into their power, waiting to transform their communities. And this book is based on that belief.

Arizmendi was just a guy, but he was a guy with a few important tools:

- He learned to *assess the deep economic burden* as the primary cause for despair and hopelessness in his community, recognizing early on that greater opportunities were the first thing needed.

- He learned to *circumnavigate existing assumptions* of community leaders and *catalyze change* on his own, after failing to convince businesses in town to hire outside their own families, by starting his own apprentice program.
- He learned to *connect people's faith with the way they lived their lives together in community,* preaching about work as our opportunity to be faithful, and our calling to care for others through teaching job skills.

Because of Arizmendi's intentional efforts, when his former pupils felt their work wasn't being honored by the traditional businesses in town, they were prepared to build their own business.

Arizmendi had some *real challenges* to his vision. The government distrusted him as a member of the Basque community, and as someone advocating for free elections. Militant nationalists distrusted him as well. The challenges that face the Mondragon Corporation today are largely the same. In an age of globalism and a challenged Spanish economic state, the low cost of goods from low-wage countries and the limited buying power of Spanish citizens are constant threats to their livelihood. The corporation has had to wrestle with issues brought to them by workers regarding gender and race prejudice. One arm of the corporation had to file for bankruptcy when their product couldn't adapt fast enough to the changing market.

And yet the Mondragon Corporation remains a model of what a company that takes care of its own can look like, a model on a huge scale that would serve any country's workers well. Arizmendi had a commitment to bringing community together and prioritizing that ethic no matter what. To this day, the Mondragon Corporation relies on the values Arizmendi taught his first trainees[3]:

1. Education of members, leaders and youth
2. Sovereignty of labor as the principal force in transforming nature, society and human life

---

3 As summarized by Ajowa Nzinga Ifateyo after a 2004 visit to Mondragon: http://www.geo.coop/node/660.

3. Subservience of capital as secondary support of the cooperative
4. Democratic organization of all workers as equals in right to knowledge, property and self-development
5. Open admission and nondiscrimination, built on respect for its constitution
6. Participation in management by employees
7. Wage solidarity through sufficient payment in line with other companies
8. Inter-cooperation among their businesses, other Basque cooperatives, and those in Spain, Europe and the rest of the world
9. Social transformation through reinvestment in new cooperative jobs and community development initiatives
10. Universal nature as "The Mondragon Co-operative Experience" declaring solidarity with all who work for economic democracy to promote peace and justice[4]

These principles are in place because one young man recognized what was wrong and brought his community together to recognize their worth and *become* the solution to their own problem. In a country facing severe financial strain, the Mondragon Corporation continues to thrive despite the modern-day struggles, even investing in developing the international co-operative movement.

The result is an obvious model for the rest of the world: the most popular bakery in my town of Oakland, CA is a cooperatively owned bakery that hires people as part-owners regardless of race, sex, gender identity, or orientation, as long as they are committed to creating a great product for the public and working in a collaborative environment of mutual respect. It borrowed from the model of Mondragon and has franchised to six worker-owned shops. (The line for pizza at their Berkeley branch, Cheese Board Pizza, can be a block long for long stretches at a time.) The name of the bakery: "*Arizmendi.*"

---

4   Ajowa Nzinga Ifateyo, "Mondragon's Corporate Model: "The Workers Have the Power," on the Grassroots Economic Organizing website, http://www.geo. coop/node/660.

I do believe there are a million Arizmendis out there, and *you* are one of them. What follows is a number of inspiring stories of communities transformed by similar changes, a discussion of the tools the change agents used, the obstacles they faced, and how their successes can be replicated using resources in your own community.

In the true spirit of Arizmendi, this book is intended to be equal parts inspiration, education, and DIY.

We'll see how a neighborhood created opportunities for self-employment and home ownership for people their city had given up on. We'll learn how restorative justice, community-driven decision-making, and truth commissions have led from conflict to harmony. And we'll be reinspired to be our neighborhood's Arizmendi, and join with the like-minded and like-hearted people all around us.

I have a history of protest and resistance, especially regarding religious tolerance, violence, racial injustice, respect for immigrants, access to housing, mistreatment of workers, and the dignity and inclusion of LGBTQ people. Much of my life's work has been protesting injustice. I have volunteered, been a "paid organizer," and mobilized my faith community to stand up against injustice. For 20 years I've been about that work at both national and local levels.

I'm also an armchair scholar of the Religious Right, and as I read the news headlines, I am reminded that this moment in U.S. history is at least partly the result of 50 years of intentional work by the Religious Right.[5] Much of that work began with local efforts, school boards, and efforts to change understandings of social issues that began local and expanded to the national arena over time.

If we are serious about creating a U.S.A. for all people, I believe we are at the beginning of a 50-year campaign. That is the work of building what we want from the ground

---

5   Nixon sought an Evangelical base for his 1968 campaign around family values. The Moral Majority came into existence just a few years later, which helped Ronald Reagan come to power. Pat Robertson's 1988 Presidential bid created the mailing list that launched the 1990s' Christian Coalition, whose rhetoric saturated the Tea Party's messaging, which helped move the country toward our current moment. Numerous books and articles point to this arc, including *Blinded by Might, God's Own Party* and *Democracy in Chains*, representing both conservative and liberal explorations of the subject.

up. I do not think it will look very much like the Religious Right's campaign because it will be both for and by a larger group of people seeking to include all people. It will also be different because it will be grounded in love, inclusion, and the possibility of redemption over only retribution and drawing the circle smaller. It *will* parallel their work in one way, though: it will start with lots of local community efforts focused on helping our communities live into a different way of relating to each other.

I have been involved in protests, marches, and rallies for public education and civil rights, and against police brutality and unfair wages. I think protests matter. Some laws and regulations only change when officials and corporate heads see enough people care about what is right and what is wrong.

But protests aren't enough. And experts can't fix communities from the outside. Only those embedded in the struggles and opportunities of their communities have the skills and the wisdom to collectively solve their problems and thrive. Only regular people like you and me can make that happen. We must spark the possibilities within ourselves, cause them to catch fire and come to life in allies around us who will make us a little less lonely in this critical work. I wrote this book so that we can all be better allies.

And I'm so excited to take the first step to becoming an *Arizmendi* with you.

1

The Power of Recognizing Assets

Everything has beauty, but not everyone can see it.

—Confucius

It is wonderful how much time good people spend fighting the devil. If they would only expend the same amount of energy loving their fellow men, the devil would die in his own tracks of ennui.

—Helen Keller

When Jason Sole walks into a prison, he brings three forms of credibility: his proven ability to effect change through organizing, his credentials as an educator at an institution of higher learning, and the fact that he knows what it's like to be incarcerated.

Jason is a motivational speaker and a consultant on reentry and juvenile justice. Part of why he gets taken seriously is that he knows what it's like to turn to a gang as a survival strategy and also to end up in the hospital and in prison for participating in a gang.

What he attributes his greatest success to, though, is using a strengths-based approach to working with youth.

So when he's talking to someone looking at 30 more years of a sentence, he will tell them, "look, man, but you're breathing. The fact that you're alive means you still have something to contribute." He'll tell the guy about how when he was in prison he'd write all the time because maybe someday someone years down the line would read his writings and be helped by them. If the guy blows him off by saying "I don't write; I play ball," he'll let them know they don't have to do it well, they just have to be willing to try it.

Jason speaks at alternative schools where kids are looking at a low likelihood of graduating from high school or going to college, and he reminds them that like him, they can go down, but they can also go up, and he points them to illustrations like Nelson Mandela as a source of hope.

And as part of his strategy, when he visits gang-affiliated youth at a juvenile detention facility, he tells the staff to come and watch as he does an exercise in which he asks youth to raise their hands in response to questions like, "How many of you wish you had your father?"

"I can relate on that basis," he explains, "so often it's that issue. And I tell the staff, 'I'll talk to them; you just pay attention so you know *why* they erupt on the floor when they feel disrespected.'"

"You get the best information from them when you do something with them rather than just sit down to talk," he explains. "I ask whether they play football, basketball, ping pong. I was at a Boys and Girls Club in Oregon, and I told this girl I had heard she was the best ping pong player and I wanted to beat her. And I really did play hard; I was sweating, and we were talking and she was saying 'I was in foster care, and I was molested, and I was emancipated at 16, and that's why I hang at the girls and boys club.' I wasn't expecting that but it was a relaxed atmosphere where I was respecting her skills and creating space for her. I said 'I have to speak to the whole group now; I want you to give me a two-minute introduction. Would you do it?' And she said, 'I don't do that,' and I said, 'let yourself stretch. I believe in you. And it would mean a lot to me since we've shared so much.' And she did, and then I talked, and afterward she said, 'I trust you.' And I didn't really know what to do with that." Sometimes the results of asset-based assessments can surprise even the person who's been using it for years.

Why Strengths-based Intervention Was Needed

As much work as Jason has done with gang members and people in prison for serious offenses, he had never planned on bringing his asset-based strategies to the community with whom he was called to work during the MIN CoSA project: sex offenders.

A Mennonite group in Canada had started an experimental project called Circles of Support and Accountability (CoSA) grounded in circle practices and built around a balance of those two things, support and accountability, for sex offenders exiting the prison and reentering the community. Recidivism had gone down, and the state of Minnesota decided to adopt the project.

"I had to learn a lot, because I had my own bias against sex offenders. But I came to learn how to provide support—someone needing a tie for a job interview, hygiene products, a ride to work, someone to talk to—with accountability. Like, I love you but I'm going to call you out if you end up in a school zone or next to a kid on a bus when you knew not to do that."

Because the project was volunteer intensive and the state would therefore focus on high-risk offenders to make their dollars stretch farther (the cost of incarcerating high-risk offenders is higher), there was significant pressure to make sure the men were supported in their pursuit of assimilating back into society and not recidivating (ending up back in prison for a violation of the constraints placed upon them upon reentry into the community). Again, the program wanted the biggest return on investment and was focusing on high-risk offenders; if they could be rehabilitated, it would save the state some real money. *If* they could be rehabilitated.

The pressure for a strengths-based approach to succeed was high; the consequences of either success or failure were very, very real.

How a Strengths-based Strategy was Employed

To ruin the suspense, MIN CoSA's research on the first four years of the program indicated a drop of 62 percent in rearrests compared to a control group. In addition, investing in the success specifically of high-risk offenders had also saved the state of Minnesota over $363,000 in that time period compared to the operating costs of a standard recidivism rate.[6]

---

6 Minnesota Department of Corrections, *An Outcome Evaluation of Minnesota Circles of Support and Accountability (MnCoSA)*, September 2012, 3–4, www.doc. state.mn.us.

In each support circle, four to seven volunteers walked with the formerly incarcerated men for a year to help them find stability. In Canada, volunteers had been primarily from church circles, but the nonprofit running the program in Minnesota had less luck with that and turned to universities. Volunteers were mostly young white women, age 21 or 22. And Jason felt again the urgency of setting up the men to succeed. He would let them know that he believed in their capacity to stay out of prison and to make a positive contribution in society. For many men, that was something they had not heard in a long time, if at all. He made sure that the volunteers and he always balanced accountability with support, and he made sure that the volunteers remained faithful to their commitment to journey with those returning citizens. They didn't meet with them alone, and they started the journey together at least four weeks before the men were preparing to exit the prison.

"Over time, those relationships became strong," Jason says, knowing that most outsiders will find that surprising. "We were all reminded of the humanity of those men. At the end-of-year picnic, people were talking and laughing; we had actually built a community of support and care in an unexpected place. And ultimately I'm not surprised; I've found that no matter who I'm working with, we can get a lot of results from starting a relationship by letting the person know, 'I'm not here to kick you; you have gifts and strengths that I know we can build on so you can succeed.'"

Strengths-based strategy is a powerful tool for working with people and communities whose gifts have historically been ignored. A good summary of strengths-based strategies from Alex Fox, CEO of the nonprofit Shared Lives is this:

> A strengths-based approach to care, support and inclusion says let's look first at what people can do with their skills and their resources and what can the people around them do in their relationships and their communities. People need to be seen as more than just their care needs—they need to be experts and in charge of their own lives.[7]

---

7 "What is a strengths-based approach to care?" The Social Care Institute for Excellence, www.scie.org.uk.

The article goes on to note that strengths-based care can tap into a client's gifts and skills that will move them forward in overcoming the obstacles in their life: "These elements include:

- their personal resources, abilities, skills, knowledge, potential, etc.
- their social network and its resources, abilities, skills, etc.
- community resources, also known as 'social capital' and/or 'universal resources'."

***

The conversations Jason has with at-risk youth, people in prison and sex offenders seeking to stay out of prison after release reflect this simple but underutilized strategy. With something as simple as telling a 16-year-old girl he knew she was the best ping pong player at the Boys and Girls Club, Jason got to connect with her on a whole different level. Honoring that gift meant he could invite her to risk being good at other things, too.

Because so much work with marginalized communities comes from a space of charity, or "us serving them," it sometimes misses a key element that solidarity brings; a "me journeying with you" alternative framework. A charity model pays attention to the needs of a client and sometimes unintentionally or unconsciously focuses on his/her limitations or failings.

The reason strengths-based strategies come naturally to Jason is he knows what a lack of support leads to, and he can still remember the moment a mentor of his (now building an eco-village in Africa) let him know he believed in Jason. His mentor asked him to talk about himself in public settings for five minutes, and then ten, and then present on a topic. "And now I do three day trainings without any stress," Jason notes.

And because he knows how someone believing in him led from him being a three-times-incarcerated gang leader to university lecturer, speaking across the country and finishing up a PhD, he sees part of his work as modeling for people that such a transformation can occur and supporting them in recognizing the innate gifts they already have that can get them to a better place.

***

Although distinct from strengths-based strategies, **asset-based community development** processes follow a similar approach. Neighborhoods that have seen a lot of disinvestment (wealthier people leaving, diminished city funding, departure of local business, decreased taxpayer-funded maintenance of public space) are often told what others will do for their neighborhood as if their role is solely to be recipients, even if their input is sought for the neighborhood development process...and oftentimes, their input *isn't* sought regarding what their neighborhood should look like.

But asset-based community development begins by looking at what gifts exist within a neighborhood. As John McKnight, community organizer and founder of Asset-Based Community Development Institute, notes, "I knew from being a neighborhood organizer that you could never change people or neighborhoods with the basic proposition that what we need to do is fix them. What made for change was communities who believed they had capacities, skills, and abilities and could create power when they came together in a community."[8]

In an article on asset-based community development, John Walker highlights a few basic keys to helping any neighborhood be its best:[9]

- Use an asset lens: look for strengths in the community.
- Be inclusive: recognize potential leadership in unexpected places and foster it.
- Map your assets: inventory the strengths you find, in ways that build trust among community members.
- Be action-oriented: move straight from assessment to tangible improvement efforts
- Let the community direct the spending (as opposed to developers or city staff)

---

8 John McKnight, "Low Income Communities are Not Needy, They Have Assets." Available online at www.faithandleadership.com
9 "Building from Strength: Asset-based community development." By John E. Walker, Northeast Assets Leadership Project. Available online at www.bostonfed.org.

- Lead by stepping back (experts can show up but not lead)
- Nurture a sense of ownership (which leads to accountability)

As communities around the country seek self-determination, asset-based community development is a tool many are using by instinct to rebuild neighborhoods devastated by decades of disinvestment and blight. Asset-based community development can also be used by those seeking to create programs for communities in need as a means of avoiding falling into the default charity (as opposed to solidarity) mode. Many well-intentioned community programs have failed due to lack of buy-in from the community the program intended to serve. Sometimes that's because the program is neither shaped by nor run in partnership with community members whose gifts remain unacknowledged because they were only seen as their needs. No individual wants to be seen as only their needs; neither does a community. And while not every person has the history or the particular gifts to coach individuals as Jason does, every person can participate in asset-based community development: it involves things like surveys and community meetings and even analyzing data; there is room for the gifts of the people person and the numbers person and the set-up-chairs person when people gather to determine the assets of their community in an intentional way so that they can effect change.

A great illustration of Asset-Based Community Development is B'more for Healthy Babies, a program to radically decrease infant mortality rates in poor communities predominantly of people of color in Baltimore. They already know how dire the statistics are related to life expectancy for infants and children in Baltimore's poorest neighborhoods; that is not where they start in their community work.

They have done surveys and community meetings. They have asked questions about what people want for their community and what they can contribute. They have asked people to surface the gifts of the community. They have helped people recognize the lies in the dominant culture accounts about their community and what the counter-narratives might be. They have made sure that mothers and their children's voices and leadership are incorporated.

B'more for Healthy Babies' work has rebuilt relationships in specific neighborhoods in Baltimore and has helped people in those communities understand the gifts they have to offer, as well as the importance of their own viewpoints about what constitutes a healthy community, so that they can advocate in front of elected officials for those priorities while building a deeper sense of community with each other. In a presentation at a conference in Edmonton, Alberta, presenters included this poem in their presentation "The Power of Conversation in Baltimore:"[10]

Poem by Afiya Ervin, grade 10
I almost forgot
about the time
I took a walk
with my sister
and admired the
artwork
on the brick walls
at the end of
every crumbling
row house.

***

There might be no better summary for the power of asset-based community development, which helps a community recognize its gifts and its power so that it can seek the good it deserves but which is so often withheld from it because no one, including the community members, has paused to recognize what is good and worth preserving in that community.

***

Jason hasn't only used strengths-based strategies with sex offenders leaving prison. He has recently been engaged in a campaign to stop the building of a juvenile prison. Elected

---

10 Powerpoint presentation available at deepeningcommunity.ca

officials had sought out $68 million dollars in funding with a goal or building a juvenile detention center. As someone invested in alternatives to incarceration for youth, Jason's thought was, "if your goal is to build a juvenile prison, your mindset is not right." The youth organizing program the Black Liberation Project had the same read as Jason. When they heard he was planning something as well, they reached out to him so that they could collaborate on a shared strategy that capitalized on all their respective gifts.

Jason brought a strengths-based strategy to supporting the voices of young people in that work, and he also imposed some asset-based community development on those elected officials.

"They said, 'we're having a community meeting to tell you how we're going to do this.' They presented their plan for half an hour and then had us in small groups. I stationed youth at every table so their stories would get heard. And then I noticed there wasn't anyone at the mic, so I took the mic and said, 'listen; we don't have a lot of time and it's really important for you to hear the stories of these youth.' And they told me I couldn't do that, but I already had, and the youth got to tell their stories of the harm that juvenile detention had done to them and the alternatives that had actually worked. The next day, the national juvenile justice expert who had come in for the meeting told me she had never seen anything like it at a community meeting; she told me we had taken power back."

Jason had made sure that the experts listened to the community and that the wisdom of the youth was honored.

He did something similar at the next two meetings and then helped the youth strategize so they could shut down the fourth meeting without him even being in the room: he acknowledged and also nurtured up the skills within them so they could take leadership over the process that would affect them. And the elected officials are no longer trying to build a juvenile detention facility.

That $68 million is still sitting there. And Jason has plans for it.

What's Happening Now

Jason recently became the president of the National Association for the Advancement of Colored People (NAACP) in Minneapolis: "I was the only male chosen to stand alongside an all-female executive committee. They made me an honorary Black woman. I'll take it!"

His plan is for the local NAACP to meet with elected officials about the future of the funds that had been planned for the juvenile detention center. He wants them to come with a strong proposal shaped by the experiences of the youth and by their own learnings: "they had their chance with the money and they lost that chance based on wanting to focus on expanding incarceration instead of programs that would stop the youth from needing to be incarcerated."

Jason's approach to leadership of the local NAACP chapter aligns with his strengths-based approach to working with anyone else. He sought out people with good hearts and commitment to the work, even if their professional credentials wouldn't normally allow them to serve in leadership positions. He has handed out books on racial justice and other issues to committee chairs with the expectation that they will reference those books in their committee reports, inviting them into a process of constantly growing and learning as part of their leadership. And when they bring him ideas, he supports them, brainstorms lots of options on how they could respond to a situation (should we have a twitter campaign? Letter writing? Press conference? Protest? Feature the issue in a webinar or talk made available online?) and then empowers them to move forward as they see fit.

Sometimes meetings can get bogged down in negativity about what went wrong with an event and why; that's when Jason invites people to pause, reflect on what they did well, and then move not to "what went wrong" but "what should we do differently." The set-up of the conversation matters as much as the content. Focusing on the positive and on how to move forward together results in better relationships and outputs.

"It's important to me that we always do things in love. That way, even if we don't achieve our goals as a branch, they take that home to their kids, their spouse or partner, people in the work place. Even if I think people dropped a big ball, I convey that I love you; we just need to figure out what to do next rather than tear you apart over it."

Jason makes sure to give others the stage now; the other night he was invited to speak at an event and instead let a 19-year-old speak about a major project he's undertaking. "I'm giving them the stage; I'm stepping back to show them I support them. As a result, they'll do that in schools and prisons and those types of situations where they're the ones with power."

These days, heading an effective civil rights organization is potentially dangerous, and Jason thinks about the movement without him. "If I don't make it, this work has to continue. I'm working to set up a culture that can carry on with or without me. It's in the spirit of the Black Lives Matter movement; we have many leaders rather than just one, and also we support each other." His words hearken to a quote by Assata Shakur that has become a common chant within the Movement for Black Lives as a reminder to extend compassion to one another as a critical element of the justice movement today: "We have a duty to fight for our freedom. We have a duty to win. We must love and support each other. We have nothing to lose but our chains."

One of the most inspiring ways Jason is going about helping the whole community lose their chains is by inviting the NAACP chapter into a maximum security prison to spend half a day with inmates, learning about the prisoners' conditions first hand, telling them what the chapter is working on to solicit input from inmates. They'll also help the inmates set up their own chapter of the NAACP in the prison. "That gives them leadership skills and a pipeline to us. So when they're coming home they can check in with the NAACP chapter in Minneapolis and we can put them on the path to success." The prison chapter of the NAACP will be spearheaded by a 24-year-old.

Jason says his goal with these projects is "so guys can come home better and not bitter." And, as with all of his work, Jason is cultivating that community by starting with the gifts people already bring to the work. This he does for the sake of his NAACP community, his prison community, and his Minneapolis community, all of which can thrive because they are daily more grounded in their strength.

LEARN MORE

Asset-based community development strategies can be used anywhere but are critical to use in communities only told of their weaknesses. They are simple (although not easy) principles to live into and can create *very* different solutions than needs-based assessments. Throughout this book you will see examples of usually ignored people recognizing their power and providing different visions for programs and movements. Asset-based efforts can result in different visions and models than needs-based efforts.

To learn more about asset-based community development and how to use tools to strengthen your own community, read John McKnight and John (Jody) Kretzmann's *Building Communities from the Inside Out: A Path Toward Finding and Mobilizing a Community's Assets*, ACTA Publications, 1993, or visit the Asset-Based Community Development Institute webpage at http://www. abcdinstitute.org. Episcopal Relief and Development also shares inspiring stories of real-life asset-based community development successes from all over the world at episcopalrelief.org.

Multiple resources for *strengths-based assessment* to use with individuals can be found at PracticeBasedEvidence.Squarespace. com and searching "Strengths Assessment Tools."

Jason's journey is movingly captured in his autobiography, *From Prison to PhD: A Memoir of Hope, Resilience, and Second Chances*, 2014. It offers inspiration and possibilities for any reader about the possibility of transformation for many people that society has given up on.

2

The Power of Listening

Community Conversations
Make a Difference

*To really belong to one another and to depend on one another—
to really share a common destiny—is difficult for a community
that wants to be diverse. It is also the community's only
hope of survival. Whether or not we will be honest with each
other, whether or not we will let ourselves be truly known,
determines everything.*

—N. GORDON COSBY

*In thinking about religion and society in the 21st century, we
should broaden the conversation about faith from doctrinal
debates to the larger question of how it might inspire us to
strengthen the bonds of belonging that redeem us from our
solitude, helping us to construct together a gracious and
generous social order*

—JONATHAN SACKS

Recovery Café San Jose stands in the shadow of the
city's massive modern glass and metal city hall. In the same
way City Hall symbolizes the abundance of Silicon Valley,
Recovery Café, with its simple Spanish colonial architecture
and a crowd of homeless people hanging out on the front
steps most days, symbolizes who and what is left in the
shadow of that abundance.

While you can generally find a cup of coffee at Recovery
Café San Jose, they offer a lot more than that: they offer hope,

and dignity, and comfort, and self-expression. The cost is a willingness to confront one's addictions...and, as Recovery Café San Jose founder Dana Bainbridge says, "we're all recovering from *something*."

Several years ago, Recovery Café San Jose was born in the building owned by First Christian Church of San Jose. Today they serve 100 regular members and around 500 distinct individuals over the course of a year. People may come for a meal and conversation; they may come for job training services or art classes or yoga or on-site transitional housing or mental health support.

But the heart of the program for those who attend are the recovery circles. "There's nothing like a person telling their story," reflects Dana. "Everyone has to be in a recovery circle to be a member. The stuff that's shared there is holy. We've had hardly any attrition. Leaders are dedicated to their recovery circles. When you step out at the end, there's nowhere else you would rather have been that last hour."

Recovery Café San Jose has only existed officially for three years at this point, and it's not surprising that it's making the lives of individuals with addictions and mental health issues better—people returning to the community after incarceration, people in transitional housing, people who are homeless, people committing to their sobriety and mental health plans. What's powerful about it, though, is it is creating a community for and by the members themselves.

"It's great to run into former members out in the community and see them doing well. Recently, I ran into a guy at the gas station who had lived in our housing program. We stay in touch with a formerly homeless guy who built our church website. He's our webmaster! Richard, who spoke so powerfully at our fundraising breakfast a couple of years ago, has gone on to lead groups at the Café, and is often out in the community meeting needs. He once was so hurt all he could do was hurt other people. Now he is passionate about giving back. He's one of the most dedicated advocates for others."

Part of the mission of Recovery Café is the implementation of a healing community model to help people deal with the traumas of homelessness, addiction, and mental health issues. Through shared meals and attending classes together and sharing stories of deep inner healing about their recovery, they begin to cultivate relationships. They may attend at first for the free meals or warm space on rainy days, but in order to be a member and get those services, a person has to show up a certain amount, and it doesn't take long to form bonds in a stable place. Members resource each other, connecting each other to more specified recovery programs elsewhere in town (like Meth Addicts or Sex and Love Addicts Anonymous). People who have been through a particular type of crisis will give their number to someone else going through the same crisis so they can support that person.

"When they removed people from all the encampments to clean up Coyote Creek in San Jose, suddenly there were a lot more people out on the sidewalks. Along with a lot of neighborhoods, we had an encampment on our street. One of the guys there used to holler at our staff and other people coming in. We just said, 'Whenever you're ready, we're here," says Dana, "One day he came in and ended up becoming a member. He's now over at the SAP Center [the city's major event venue] doing staffing for events there. And he hires our people. Because someone from our program gave him a chance, he gives others a chance." Sometimes after people have jobs and housing and can't come back to the daytime programs, they'll still drop in after work. In the shadow of City Hall, Recovery Café San Jose has created a community of people who look different from the people working next door but who are just as deserving of dignity. Most of the people who work there know it. In fact, the City Housing Department has now given RCSJ a grant to renovate the building so that they can expand their programs.

Why Recovery Café San Jose Came into Being

According to the National Coalition for the Homeless, 36 percent of people living on the street have an alcohol addiction and 28 percent regularly use another substance such as drugs.[11] The Coalition cites a 2008 survey of the U.S. Conference of Mayors in which 28 percent of cities surveyed listed substance abuse treatment as one of the top three items needed to combat homelessness.

Homelessness, mental health issues, and addiction weave a complex web that mean addressing only one is insufficient to support the well-being of any individual dealing with all three. Especially for individuals without access to prescription medication, street drugs and alcohol often serve as self-medication for people dealing with the trauma of homelessness and other traumas such as abuse or PTSD.

First Christian Church of San Jose had the heart for this work long before Dana arrived as their pastor in 2009. Their mission statement was (and is) "To be a church in recovery from and resistance to the dominant culture and to bring the kingdom of God here and now." It was a church that had created space in worship for people who were homeless, who drank, and who had mental health issues that might disrupt worship. They already had an informal emergency family shelter in the building. The church did not need to be convinced that they should play a role in supporting homeless people. The church already understood that we're all in recovery from something, including recovery from a culture that honors greed and profit above the well-being of the people with the fewest opportunities and the least hope. And the church understood that dealing with homelessness was about more than finding people homes; it was about caring for the whole person and creating community in the face of a system that did not provide enough of any of those supports.

---

11 "Substance Abuse and Homelessness" National Coalition for the Homeless, July 2009, available at http://www.nationalhomeless.org/factsheets/addiction. pdf. The policy paper goes on to say "For many homeless people, substance abuse co-occurs with mental illness. Often, people with untreated mental illnesses use street drugs as an inappropriate form of self-medication. Homeless people with both substance disorders and mental illness experience additional obstacles to recovery, such as increased risk for violence and victimization and frequent cycling between the streets, jails, and emergency rooms (Fisher and Roget, 2009). Sadly, these people are often unable to find treatment facilities that will help them. Many programs for homeless people with mental illnesses do not accept people with substance abuse disorders, and many programs for homeless substance abusers do not treat people with mental illnesses."

Simultaneously, in Dana's previous church, she had been invited to Alcoholics Anonymous meetings by members of her church who thought every pastor should experience the 12 steps. She recognized something like church but more powerful in her first meeting: spiritual surrender, community support, and people who said it had saved their lives. So she was already "looking deeply," as Zen master Thich Nhat Hanh says, for how to be present with what's with us in ways that are spiritually transformative.

And beyond that she was also asking, "how do you create structures, as Gordon Cosby says, that people can step into and be part of? Not just what *you* want but what *they* would want to step into. The church today is not a structure most people want to step into."

So when the church and the pastor came together, the seeds of Recovery Café San Jose had already been planted.

The Challenges Recovery Café San Jose Faced

The church's greatest gift was also one of its greatest challenges. The church had for a number of years hosted an emergency family shelter and had gone to battle over whether the shelter could legally stay in that space. Those battles had sometimes been with the city and sometimes with the neighbors.

In addition, people were giving their whole hearts to the work of providing emergency shelter but were not able to get much traction with helping people move into a better life. The housing situation was, and is, dire. So it takes a lot of resources, patience, and skill to move people from homelessness to housing. The shelter was run with tenacious faith and dedication and a sense of justice, but it was not safe. Some people did get hurt, and it was not for the most part moving people out of homelessness.

The church, after Dana's arrival, made some changes to make their ministry to the homeless more relational so they would get to know the homeless people in their space or the people eating meals there instead of just opening their doors. "The heartbreaking thing was that as we got to know people, we watched them die," said Dana. "I recently heard

Meryl Streep say that when we see heartbreak, it can be an opportunity for action. Well, there was so much heartbreak, what were we going to do about it?"

The church held a memorial service for Frank, a man who would sit and drink in front of the building and would only ever sit in the back pew because he didn't think as an alcoholic he deserved to be closer to the front. At the memorial service, family from all over the country came and told stories about how much they had loved him, and we got to see another chapter of Roger's life before his disease progressed. How he'd been part of a family, had a job, and lots of good memories too. There was far more to him than just a humble homeless alcoholic who died on a park bench.

Within weeks, two more people died, one of them on the steps of the church. "This isn't working," Dana thought; "I can't do this, this loving them and watching them die." They were working hard, serving almost 600 meals a week, yet hardly anyone was getting better.

Community churches were deeply invested in the shelter and feeding program in downtown San Jose, and a sister congregation in the building took the lead in much of the existing homeless ministry. That may seem like a blessing, but it was another challenge. The church faced three challenges: their ministry to homeless people had alienated them from both their neighbors and some elected officials; the more they got to know the people they served, the clearer it was that what they were doing wasn't enough; and there were people they had journeyed with for years who were deeply invested in the ministry exactly as it was.

Why It Worked

For big picture and strategic thinkers, two important elements to Recovery Café San Jose's success are helpful to know. First is the model RCSJ borrowed from and got buy-in on, and second is how they funded the ministry.

In Washington, D.C., there exists a church famous among progressive Christians looking for alternatives to traditional church. It might be described as the Anti-

Megachurch: Church of the Saviour. Founded by a World War II army chaplain who became disillusioned with war and became committed to deepening relationships across racial divides, Church of the Saviour has spawned dozens of nonprofits and has rejected the growth of their original church much beyond 100 people, instead launching new faith communities based on the same loose model: projects are started by regular people responding to the need they see in the community. The voices of impacted communities help shape those ministries (homeless people shaping homeless ministries, jobless people shaping job training program goals, etc.).

One of their offshoots was the original Recovery Café in Seattle. Dana was inspired by the model and saw it as replicable. So she took people there in groups of five or six to see it in action—people from the church but also people from the wider community, many of whom became part of RCSJ's launch team. After a critical mass of congregants and community members were sold on the project, they brought down the leaders of Recovery Café to meet with all sorts of people: funders; city officials, church members, and nonprofit agencies. A large group meeting included conversation and Q&A. Killian Noe, the Seattle Recovery Café Founder, shared the model and told stories. A private meeting with church folks allowed them to share how they were feeling about the church transforming the building into a Recovery Café of their own. "A few were concerned the church was throwing all their eggs in one basket. But they got to say their piece and felt heard and respected, and they got to a place where they chose not to get in the way. Which was really generous on their part. And they stayed the course, holding other aspects of the church's life together."

So there was enough energy to launch RCSJ. But energy is not the same thing as money. And "without money, there could be no programs." Jim Thompson, one of the co-founders would say this often. Even though he was fundraising for his own nonprofit, he was infinitely available to support early and ongoing fundraising efforts. His wisdom about fundraising and leadership was invaluable. He brought a few donors to the table, and when it was a key fundraising moment, he was always there to add wise counsel. The team of RCSJ enthusiasts worked for six months to host a breakfast at a downtown venue. They got 250 people there, including potential high level donors who wouldn't come to the church but would come to a well-known event space to learn about the project. They brought Killian down from Seattle again to speak at the breakfast, and they raised $60,000. Government officials came, were inspired, and started looking out for grants for the program. People who attended gave when approached closer to the launch date. A grant and a couple of major donations later, and they had a little over $200,000—18 months' worth of funding according to the budget in their business model. That effort reached people who may never visit RCSJ but understood the need for it. It was enough to start something and was substantial enough to have the potential to build capacity.

But that's not all it takes to launch a project like RCSJ, especially given the history the congregation had in the community (a proud and faithful history of standing with homeless people, but a history that potentially created resistance to a pretty remarkable project).

One Tool RCSJ Used to Transcend Challenges

Irish comedian Dylan Moran once said, "The measure of a conversation is how much mutual recognition there is in it; how much shared there is in it. If you're talking about what's in your own head, or without thought to what people looking and listening will feel, you might as well be in a room talking to yourself."

As many technical aspects as there were to the launch of RCSJ, and as many skills as the leadership team needed, they would never have gotten to that point without conversations: one-to-one conversations, community conversations, and painful conversations.

They had to have hard conversations with the church that had been so engaged in their previous homeless ministry. (That church has moved locations and continues to do work with homeless people in need of emergency support.) They had honest conversation with churches from the suburbs who had been running meal programs, who were irate at a church ending a ministry of care. "We said, 'come with us and do this Recovery Café thing with us; we'll be doing the same thing but very differently. We believe it will help more people more substantively,'" said Dana. "One of the churches eventually came back and helps us with work projects, but there was a time they were all hurt. Those were not easy moments."

I wanted to interview Dana about a conversation model the church used called "World Café." (A little confusing, to be sure; World Café conversation model at the physical place called Recovery Café.) Interestingly enough, Dana said she doesn't see that model as foundational to the launch of RCSJ, and she attributes it more to a community organizing skill called "one-to-ones," basically conversations with individuals that allow you to understand that person's concerns, level of investment and power or resources.

Since I think community organizing, one-to-ones, and the process that resulted in the use of the World Café model tell a lot about an essential soft skill that allowed the church to overcome the challenges they faced, I'd like to share a little of the story with you.

Before the church had even begun talking about Recovery Café, they began engaging in community organizing as a way of more effectively engaging the systemic issues they saw harming their friends who were homeless. The church was involved with a community organizing group called PACT, People Acting in Community Together, an affiliate of the PICO National Network. Two members of First Christian, Sandra Hietala and Jim Thompson, had a son who wrote books on community organizing and he came by his passions honestly, through the dedication of his parents to social justice. Sandra, who would think of herself as a layperson who shouldn't be out front, headed up FCC's local organizing committee with PACT. She was passionate and relentless in following up and keeping things moving. When Sandy believed in something, she talked to everyone about it and was often recruiting people to be involved. Through a series of one-to-ones with community members, their congregational PACT local organizing committee had determined that their focus would be public transit. The churches in the local organizing committee continually got calls saying, "Do you have help with bus passes?"

A professor at a nearby university had her students join up with the people from PACT to do some intensive research on "Hotel 22," a bus that goes from San Jose to Palo Alto, which some homeless people would ride all night long. PACT members became the researchers, hanging out at bus stops and doing surveys and hearing people's stories. "It's that thing that grows out of listening," says Dana; "that whole listening thing is so huge. People went into new places and were listening and trying to figure out what to do with those stories and what they mean." Those surveys were another form of one-to-ones.

One-to-ones had gotten them their focus on transit issues for poor people, and it had gotten them data on the specific problems facing homeless people in particular. The one-to-ones and the "research" that are part of community organizing had gotten them comfortable asking for meetings with public officials, community partners, anyone who had information about issues. In that process they learned that people will meet with you if you're interested in solving public problems. But to get the right power brokers talking to each other and hearing the stories that had moved the members of PACT would require a different model.

First Christian Church of San Jose had used the World Café model early in Dana's tenure to build relationships among three congregations sharing space at First Christian Church of San Jose, so that across their cultural and theological differences, the members of the three churches could build up empathy and understanding of one another. The transit project seemed like a good opportunity to use the model again.

The World Café process is designed around seven basic principles that "help people have conversations that matter." It is adaptable to many contexts with the goal being to create an environment that allows for small group dialogue, cross pollination, questions that help move attendees towards the desired purpose of the Café, harvesting of insights, and graphic recording of the results. When it's done well, it's remarkable how by the end of three rounds of questions with people changing their tables for each round, many groups have found some common ground in collective wisdom that emerged for common recommendations for next steps. Also amazing is how a sense of intimacy can occur in a room of dozens or even hundreds of people.

PACT gathered Valley Transit Association high-level staff, public officials and their staff, social workers, homeless people, and people of faith. They framed the issue and offered a series of carefully worded questions which people discussed in small groups, changing tables before each new question, so that their conversation partners changed and they carried wisdom from the previous group into the new group. During one table discussion, the question posed was "What can we do to ensure that every downtown (San Jose) homeless person who wants to get to essential services can get there?" A VTA staff person concurred that the focus should be on "essential services" as the only passes (assuming that there was agreement about his interpretation of what constituted "essential services").

One of the women at his table asked, "Who are you to say what is an essential service for me?" then continued, "the problem is I need a voucher that will allow me to take my kids from the shelter safely to school across town and then to the community college where I'm studying so I can eventually get us out of homelessness. And that kind of voucher doesn't exist, because I'm only allowed to go to and from work."

In his years of planning, the staff person hadn't had the chance to hear directly from someone his programs served about what the limitations of the program were and how they could better serve the people they intended to serve.

At least, not in this way. Since he had never been a homeless mother trying to get an education, he didn't know from experience. VTA has "public hearings," but the World Café model put people on an equal level around small tables of 4. It's such a different experience than a public hearing. A World Café including an intentional mixture of people with institutional power and people with lived experience around the issue at hand helped him recognize how the program would need to change. This is the beauty of the World Café principle of "collective wisdom" where our wisdom is better in dialogue with each other instead of the current paradigm of individualism. Through this model, new solutions can emerge through collective wisdom that could never have occurred with just one person (or staff) puzzling out a solution in isolation.[12]

***

During our conversation, Dana said that the World Café didn't have a lot to do with RCSJ's formation, although she did comment that she thinks community organizers could use the World Café process more often, and more effectively. She added, "I'm definitely not against demonstrations but so often all we do is yell at each other. These days I'm less interested in demonstrations and more interested in getting people who don't talk to each other to talk to each other civilly in ways that move people towards action. World Café is phenomenal in that regard."

She commented that one-to-one organizing is still essential and will be part of making the community dialogues happen. "One-on-one conversations in mass numbers add up to relational capital. A big piece is we try to build relational capital to deal with these conflict issues and to build support in the community for all the help we need to do it: engagement, funding, human resources, volunteers."

---

12 Special thanks to friend and colleague Paula Pociecha, who has facilitated many world cafes as well as having done doctoral work around World Café as a conversation model. Paula attended this particular World Café, thus filling in critical details and re-grounding the beauty of the World Café model in its collective wisdom framework…we create better when informed by each other's wisdom, and what we co-create is so rich!

One of their early partners was Downtown Streets Team, a program that provides jobs to the street community and seeks to move them directly into permanent housing. When the church entered the rezoning process to have legal transitional housing and new programs on site, they were required by the City to spend a couple of thousand dollars mailing information to their neighbors about a community meeting. The City has to have input from your neighborhood if you want to rezone something. "[The previous homeless ministry] had alienated a lot of people at City Hall, as well as neighbors and we knew people were going to show up and say 'hey; they were building bonfires in the parking lot,'" said Dana. "We knew we needed to meet with those people first. We shouldn't wait for them to show up and say that at a public meeting. We needed to listen, and address their concerns. Downtown Streets Team is such an amazing, positive, uplifting program. We took DST members to neighborhood association meetings and had them share their stories about going from living on the street, to working, feeling empowered and encouraged, having the dignity of being part of the solution. We would explain that it's these people who are working who are going to be living in our housing now. It's going to be good for the neighborhood. One night, I finally left one of those meetings because the neighbors were enjoying their conversations with DST members and it was late. I said, 'I gotta go to bed' and left them to it."

From Dana's vantage point, the one-to-one meetings that preceded community meetings were at least as important as the community meetings themselves. She mentioned a man, who likes to think of himself as curmudgeonly, who owns most of the buildings on the church's block. He originally thought their proposal was atrocious. Dana has breakfast with him regularly. She listens and talks with him and they tease each other about their radically different political stances. At this point he's a grudging supporter of—and even occasional donor to—their work.

The running thread of the World Café and one-to-one meetings and community meetings that played a role in the church's engagement with systemic issues (from transit justice to zoning to avoiding neighborhood efforts to shut down their program) is *listening*. For the people wanting to effect change, it meant listening to the people who would be affected by the changes. For people in power, it meant listening to the people affected by their decisions. For Dana, it means listening to the longtime residents and the members of RCSJ and helping them find shared solutions to their problems. It doesn't necessarily mean giving all voices the same exact weight: poor people's voices are already listened to less, and if there are moments their voices can be amplified to balance the voices of people in positions of power, that might create more equity. With that caveat, creating spaces to listen has strategic benefits (who will support my plan, and what skills will they bring?), but it also builds a different type of community, a community shaped by the people it intends to serve in ways that inspire and energize the people in the neighborhood. Not every problem has a solution that is win-win, but the people who created RCSJ discovered that with enough avenues for listening, far more problems have a win-win solution than we are led to believe.

Where They Are Now

The thing that shouldn't be ignored in the telling of Recovery Café San Jose's story is the same thing that shouldn't be missed in Recovery Café Seattle's or Church of the Saviour's stories: the intersections of addiction, mental health issues, poverty, and lack of access to affordable housing. All of these organizations have to invest time on multiple fronts because the lack of access to mental health services and lack of access to affordable housing make addressing addiction and recovery that much harder even while they are that much more necessary.

"Recovery is intricately connected to behavioral health," notes Dana. "That is a dominant challenge now because our country is woefully inadequate at addressing mental health issues. We have a certain standard for cancer care. But our investment in providing excellent, high quality mental health care doesn't even begin to compare. It's not even in the same ballpark in terms of values."

The church remains involved in PACT so that they can continue to pay attention to systemic justice issues and policy solutions. But given the landscape in which they exist, RCSJ continues to do that work at the intersection of housing insecurity, mental health and addiction until systems are created that provide housing as a human right across the country.

RCSJ is now established as a nonprofit organization separate from the church and requires no particular faith tradition to participate, *and* members of the church remain active in it, both of which seem critical to its forward movement. RCSJ has a board of 12 people all asked to raise $10,000 per year to support RCSJ's budget. It has a program that serves 100 members on a regular basis and up to 500 people a year, a staff of three full-time, four part-time, and two volunteer staff.

RCSJ was one of the first replicas of Seattle's Recovery Café in 2014, but the idea is catching on and five more are starting on the West Coast with others across the country. There is now a certification process and in June 2016, Dana and others from RCSJ attended their first affiliate cohort.

"I think recovery requires the deepest inner transformation of any process," says Dana. "The people who step into their process of recovery keep stepping into it. They are some of the most resilient, courageous people in the world...they're more real. Nobody's trying to pretend they're something they're not most of the time. They are incredibly real people to be with."

An unofficial mantra at RCSJ, a de-stigmatizing mantra in a world that stigmatizes certain kinds of addictions (and criminalizes some based on race and class[13]), is "we're all in recovery from something."

Dana recognizes that some of the power of RCSJ's work is not just listening, but having listened, saying something. "By calling ourselves Recovery Café, we're participating in destigmatizing addiction so we can actually help people recover from addiction. It's not Anonymous and tucked away in a basement. It's right there on the sign at the front

---

13 If you have not yet read Michelle Alexander's book *The New Jim Crow*, you are missing out on one of the most important works of our era.

door. Some addictions are more stigmatized than others: "Killian calls work-a-holism America's most celebrated addiction. I loved that even the Mayor of San Jose stood up at our fundraising breakfast and said, 'as we all start to look at our own addictions, we realize we all need support for this journey in our lives.' It's so affirming and community-building when our leaders speak like this. Stigmas kill, so we're removing the stigma in order to treat the struggle."

LEARN MORE

RCSJ is grounded is some excellent community organizing principles, and *learning how to do one-to-one conversations* is a critical element of creating solutions that represent the passions and commitments of the community. There are many books on community organizing, but a good one was written by Gabriel Thompson, son of Recovery Cafe SJ's two other Founding Directors, Sandra Hietala and Jim Thompson. Gabriel has written a concise and clear introduction "Calling All Radicals: How Grassroots Organizing Can Save Our Democracy" Also, a very simple introduction to one-to-one meetings can be found at the Joint Religious Legislative Committee's website JRLC.org by searching "introduction to community organizing." You can also check out Training for Change's "technical instruction guide" at NewJimCrowOrganizing.org.

When a community feels stuck or at an impasse, or when building up connection is critical to the next step of a community's work, hosting a World Café with a cross section of people can help solutions emerge that people could never have discovered on their own. A basic guide for hosting a World Café can be found on the organization's website at TheWorldCafe.com (search "hosting tool kit"). The guide explains the roles of aesthetics and creativity and cross-pollination in fostering up a meaningful dialogue for 15 or 150. World Café also has a book available with stories of how the model has been used all over the world: *The World Café: Shaping Our Futures Through Conversations That Matter*, published in 2005. Imagine a conversation that allowed a homeless single mother to help a high-level transit staff person rethink how public transit could better serve people who need it most. Now imagine who should be in conversation in your community. Bring them together for this kind of dialogue.

If you're interested in exploring the Recovery Café model, Killian Noe now has a book on Recovery Café called *Descent into Love*, published 2015. You can also learn more about the affiliate program at Recoverycafe.org/about/share-our-model. If we are all in recovery from something, we need more spaces where the stigma of addiction is rejected in favor of conversation and behavioral support that lead to healing and thriving.

3

The Power of Making Things Right

Restorative Justice Models

In a real sense all life is interrelated. All men are caught in an inescapable network of mutuality, tied in a single garment of destiny. Whatever affects one directly, affects all indirectly. I can never be what I ought to be until you are what you ought to be, and you can never be what you ought to be until I am what I ought to be...This is the interrelated structure of reality.

—Rev. Dr. Martin Luther King, Jr.

What kind of society spends more on cages than classrooms?

—Rep. Pete Lee (Colorado)

In 1995, Sharletta Evans's three-year-old son Casson Xavier Evans, nicknamed Biscuit, was killed in a drive-by shooting. The three shooters were teenagers. Evans had to endure three separate trials.

"As we look back on the photographs of Paul [one of the three youth sentenced for Casson's death] walking through the courthouse he has this smirk on his face like he could care less what he had done," said Evans. "And that smirk on his face is the image I've had of Paul Littlejohn for the last 21 years."

Evans's journey had already led her to become an advocate opposed to life sentences for teenagers, and because the state of Colorado had recently adopted a statewide victim-offender mediation program commonly known as Restorative Justice, she had met with another of the men who had killed her son before meeting Paul.

"Having that four-hour victim-offender dialogue," said Evans, "he changed that image I had of him."

When Evans met with Raymond, another of the men in prison for her son's murder, she had a blunt conversation with him that weaved between transparent anger and wondering what God's plan was in the midst of this. And towards the end of their meeting, she decided she was ready to physically connect: she asked him to extend his arms and turn his palms up; she took his hands and prayed:

"I prayed that they would cause no more harm, that they'd be hands of comfort, that they would bring help and serve people and that they would no longer be hands of destruction but hands that bring life."

Hearing his confession and extending forgiveness, both Evans and her son Calvin Hurd (who was six when his brother was killed) believed Raymond had experienced both transformation and remorse. And they experienced a different level of healing than they had found up to that point.[14]

Why Restorative Justice Is Needed

The current justice system around the world (often referred to as retributive justice because it is set up around specific laws and consequences for violating those laws) is a few hundred years old at this point. It has been around long enough for most of us to take it for granted, and for some of us to miss the fact that its retribution is not equally dispersed or that its results are less than stellar.

Disparate sentencing based on race and class has become a common subject of discussion in some circles.[15] The higher likelihood of an innocent person ending up on death row

---

14 This story comes from both the article and the accompanying video by the *Denver Post:* Kevin Simpson, "Denver woman feels the power of restorative justice after son murdered, July 9, 2012, www.denverpost.com.

15 Michelle Alexander's book *The New Jim Crow* spurred a great deal of conversation on this subject when it was released in 2010, although the Supreme Court case Kimbrough v. United States in 2007 had already pointed out that across the country, people went to prison for longer terms for possession of the same amount of crack versus cocaine, which correlated to steeper sentencing of poor people and Black people in comparison to wealthier people and white people. Additionally, James Forman Jr's book *Locking Up Our Own* eloquently lays out the creative ways we can establish alternatives to a system that serves neither victim nor offender (nor society) well.

if they are Black was heartrendingly detailed in Bryan Stevenson's book *Just Mercy*. And the phrase "school-to-prison pipeline" (which some have renamed the cradle-to-prison pipeline) points to how some children are more likely to be suspended for disciplinary issues based on race, and suspension rates correlate to juvenile detention and to long prison records.[16]

One article on restorative justice notes, "Statistically speaking, high school dropouts are much more likely to become incarcerated than those who graduate. According to a 2006 study by the Alliance for Excellent Education, a national policy and advocacy organization, 75 percent of America's state prison inmates, 59 percent of federal inmates and 69 percent of jail inmates in America do not have high school diplomas. In California, youth recidivism—the rate at which youths return to prison—runs as high as 90 percent. Youth completing restorative justice programs, however, have a significantly lower recidivism rate, in the range of only 10 to 20 percent."[17]

The current retributive justice system certainly hurts people because it is unjustly implemented. It also misses an element that many ancient indigenous justice practices included: in focusing on laws broken, it does not connect the crime to the victim, and it does not truly and deeply honor the experience of the victim.

For years, this system has seemed inadequate to people on all sides. And so began to emerge an alternative.

How Restorative Justice Emerged

Restorative justice has actually existed in various forms for thousands of years within various indigenous communities; in fact, according to the Canadian Department of Justice, "the continued overrepresentation of Aboriginal peoples in correctional institutions in Canada has led to demands for

---

16 The *Christian Science Monitor* discussed this issue in the March 31, 2013 cover story by Stacy Teicher Khadaroo, "School Suspensions: Does racial bias feed the school-to-prison pipeline?"

17 Eric K. Arnold, "Oakland leads way as restorative justice techniques enter education mainstream," Center for Public Integrity, July 11, 2012, www.publicintegrity.org.

more traditional approaches, such as sentencing circles, for Aboriginal offenders."[18] So it is probably not surprising that the first major victim-offender mediation circle attributed to the burgeoning restorative justice movement occurred in Canada in 1974.

Since that time, it has moved from Canada around the world, including now having deep roots in both Chicago and Oakland, two cities known for their violence and with an urgent desire to change that reality. It is no longer solely the domain of prisons and jails and is found in schools and neighborhoods as well, with a dream of creating lasting solutions to violence by reducing recidivism and reducing the likelihood of acting out or of punishing in ways that don't move a person towards a better way of being.

How Restorative Justice Works

Teresa Frisbie, director of the Loyola University Chicago School of Law Dispute Resolution Program, tells the following story: Two youth in Des Moines, Iowa were caught spray painting swastikas on a synagogue. Members of the synagogue called for the judge to throw the book at the youth for their heinous crime. The attorney asked the rabbi if the members would be willing to sit down with the youth to try a restorative justice process, and to the rabbi's surprise, after some serious debate and discussion, the members of the synagogue agreed.

The youth met Holocaust survivors who had gone into hiding after the tagging of the synagogue. They explained to the youth the horrors of the extermination camps and what that symbol had done to their families.

The synagogue members learned that one of the youth had been seriously bullied throughout childhood in part due to hearing loss and speech problems. The Aryan Nation, recognizing his vulnerability, recruited, embraced and mentored him with the goal of him becoming a leader in his hometown and recruiting other white supremacists. His only recruit was a young and willing girlfriend along for the ride.

---

18 "The Effects of Restorative Justice Programming: A Review of the Emprirical." Canada Department of Justice, www.justice.gc.ca.

Over the course of hours they began to recognize one another's humanity and one another's fear. In that way, "they were able to craft a solution whereby the young couple acknowledged what they had done and agreed to perform restitution by spending many hours cleaning the building and studying Jewish history, including the history of persecution." The agreement also included getting GEDs, Nazi tattoo removal and the temple getting the young man a hearing specialist.[19]

Restorative justice was the domain of prisons and juvenile detention facilities for many years, but it is now showing up in school districts and neighborhood groups and in family counseling as a means of restoring broken relationships when conflicts seem intractable. In schools, RJ is reducing detentions and suspensions, but it is also changing the culture of schoolyards and playgrounds, because inherent in the model is cultivating empathy when that seems hard to do, and claiming accountability when that also seems hard to do.

In a four-part series on the violence in Chicago, Cheryl Graves reflected that restorative justice is the only hope she sees for reducing violence, and that's from an expert location:

> "Gun law debates in Congress are one thing," says Cheryl Graves, founder of the Community Justice for Youth (CJYI), "but that won't really impact what happens on the street here." Cheryl worked for years as a trial attorney, and "I loved my work; loved the performance aspect of trial law. But it was an endless cycle of repetitive cases, with no reduction in crime. The system just doesn't change" through court and prison justice, she insists. Launching CJYI "to save lives and keep kids out of the court system" and in school, service programs, and jobs, Cheryl and her team have trained over 5,000 people in restorative justice. They've trained people from Kenya (ahead of their 2013 presidential elections) to Chicago. "We'll train people in circle-work wherever they go—the

---

19 Teresa F. Frisbie: "Restorative Justice is expanding in Illinois, but more can still be done," *Chicago Daily Law Bulletin*, Monday, July 28, 2014.

barber shop, beauticians, the old grandma who lets kids sit on her front steps after school," she explains.[20]

Believing that "hurt people hurt people," Graves and her colleague Father Dave Kelly of Precious Blood Ministry of Reconciliation work at helping gang members and formerly incarcerated youth cultivate the accountability and respect that will help them eventually thrive and heal. That means being in RJ circles with members of opposing gangs and families who have been hurt by that person's crime. Real dialogue like that cannot happen in the court system which is built around accountability to laws rather than accountability to people.

Whether in prison or a school or a neighborhood meeting, RJ orients itself generally around three main questions:

- Who has been hurt?
- What are their needs?
- Whose obligations are these?

Establishing the process involves a lot of set up, so this isn't a model that people can just jump into, explains CamishaFatimah Gentry, a restorative justice consultant who worked for many years with Restorative Justice for Oakland Youth, considered to be one of the flagship programs in the nation for restorative justice in public schools. CamishaFatimah watched the program grow from 2 staff to 40 with a current goal of being present in every single public school in Oakland from high school down to elementary. "You start with buy in, then you implement the circles (where participants speak their lived experiences) really well, then you follow up," she says. The reason she is inspired by it is it invites all people to pay attention to why they react to situations in the way they do and to recognize that in each other as well, with a goal of being able to be better to one another and also be better human beings. "It is true with almost every person I've dealt with: how we respond to the world is rooted in how we were raised. We have to become aware of that in order to do the work necessary to heal."

20 Suzanne Skees, "'Gun Laws Won't Impact Us Here' in the Line of Fire, Say Peace Workers: Part 1 of 4," *Huffington Post*, September 28, 2013, www.huffingtonpost. com.

The community buy-in that CamishaFatimah mentions is not just important for promotional purposes; it matters because otherwise the community will not actually change, even if the whole school is engaged. During a panel on the 10th anniversary of restorative justice work in Chicago, Cheryl Graves made the following observation:

> [Some years back] there was a lot of energy from systems people to move the restorative justice agenda in North Lawndale. There were also social service providers on board, but there weren't that many community people. And so that initiative had systems energy, but it didn't have community energy. Things began to happen, but they didn't really gel until maybe 4 or 5 years later when the community said, "You know what, this restorative justice stuff, there's something to it. We need it because too many of our kids are getting arrested, too many of our kids are getting expelled. They're getting arrested in schools." The community then had that foundation to build upon. And now we've got community people who've been trained in victim offender conferencing, who've been trained in peer jury, who've been trained in peace-making circles, who actually now even have an entity in North Lawndale, Sankofa, which is hearing something like 40 or 50 cases a month of North Lawndale kids. Instead of them going into the system, they've been diverted out.[21]

CamishaFatimah also notes that restorative justice serves all parties, including the part that most people balk at: forgiveness. "Forgiveness is a gift for the person receiving and giving. Letting go happens in that process; it softens the heart and also empowers the person to move forward. Softening the heart is actually part of empowerment."

---

21 Cheryl Graves, "AREA Dialogue: Towards a Restorative Justice City: Ten years and counting" (areachicago.org).

The Greatest Challenge to Restorative Justice

Obviously, skepticism is a major barrier to restorative justice making its way throughout the U.S. criminal justice system (although many guards, wardens, chaplains, probation officers and police are so aware of the failings of the existing system they can be very open to alternatives like RJ). Politicians' desire to be perceived as "tough on crime" creates another barrier, especially when paired with media coverage that inaccurately suggests crime is growing when in fact it is decreasing in all but a few major cities. But CamishaFatimah notes that the greatest challenge is with people going on the restorative justice journey themselves.

The ongoing challenge of restorative justice, she notes, is that people may believe themselves to be open and ready for the process but then in fact resist it. "People say they want to do the work. They begin to do the work. But oftentimes they do not follow through because of the level of awareness, reflection and character changes that have to remain present in our daily walk." She said that this is actually one of the biggest barriers to success and saturation of restorative justice in the field, an issue that practitioners of restorative justice actively bemoan when they gather.

"It's not easy, and you have to be willing to be uncomfortable, be aware that you'll get defensive or rationalize behavior and have to deal with that. It requires working with the uncomfortable parts of ourselves to become more comfortable with our authentic selves."

And that is actually the payoff, so hard to get to: finally getting to be our authentic selves.

What This Community Looks Like as a Result

In reports from the Longmont (CO) Police Department's Restorative Justice Programs and the Longmont Community Justice Partnership, Master Police Officer Greg Ruprecht states that youth programs show exponential drops in recidivism (at this writing the rate is 10 percent, compared to 60-70 percent nationwide) and high participant satisfaction. Perhaps even more poignant is the tens of thousands of dollars, per case, that is saved from diverting youth from incarceration. In a recent live interview Officer Ruprecht shared his initial doubts about Restorative Justice, coming from a background as a Veteran serving in the Army, he says he was very skeptical at first. And then he saw it in action. To the argument that it "has no teeth" he responded, "it actually has more teeth" and that having to face one's crime and do that truthfully is much harder than being locked away.[22]

One of the purposes of this book is to look at how communities are growing stronger through the various models people are using, rather than only paying attention to personal improvement. Obviously individuals who stay out of prison and become contributing members of society have a better quality of life, and people who are able to find peace with their loss and heal through both forgiveness and the experience of their assailant's remorse likewise have better lives. Communities where the retributive justice system has torn apart families will, over time, experience a strengthening of community as this model becomes more deeply entrenched. That said, it is too soon to see the flourishing of that in neighborhoods dealing with so many other traumas still, especially when it takes years to normalize a culture of restorative justice so that it permeates family and school and religious community and street life as well as prisons and jails.

But there is a community burgeoning in an unexpected place, according to CamishaFatimah: "With all the shifting and changing in the people we work with, it takes 7-10 years to make a significant shift. Teachers leave, people are homeless and moving because of gentrification. It's so hard to keep track of folks; we're constantly starting over. The thing is, though, when I started, there were one or two people in the whole city I could turn to for wisdom and advice. Now there's a huge network and system of people doing the work

---

22 Molly Rowan Leach, "Restorative Justice Is On the Rise," *Huffington Post*, July 23, 2013, www.huffingtonpost.com.

in and out of the city; there's a huge network of very diverse people doing this work in all kinds of places, supporting each other and resourcing each other because we have this shared vision. When we talk about building community, that's the strength and community for me."

Marge Piercy's famous poem "The Low Road" ends with the stanza,

It goes on one at a time,
it starts when you care
to act, it starts when you do
it again after they said no,
it starts when you say We
and know who you mean, and each
day you mean one more

***

The restorative justice movement is building that community where each day they mean one more.

And restorative justice is simultaneously deeply personal. CamishaFatimah came to the work because of her passion for self-development. She believes in "the power of being heard, the power of forgiving, restoring myself back to my original self; the Arabic term is fitrah, the original way you came here before it was mediated through the place you were born and your family upbringing and society's influences. I am about returning to that.

"Being a product of our environment can hold us in harmful ways but also in beautiful ways," she clarifies. "Restorative justice gives us an avenue and philosophy to live ongoing in a state of shifting to our better selves, our original selves so we can peel the onion layers back and stand up for what we believe in a powerful way where we're not bullying or intimidating, where we're not causing more violence or harm but we're leading others who may not be as courageous to guide them back to their original selves. It's about how to be human, learning and relearning how to be, how to build."

Charletta Evans, who lost her three-year-old son in 1995 in Colorado, regained herself through the restorative justice process where she prayed over a man involved in her son's murder. "What I got for myself was that I have a sense of more feeling who Charletta is, my identity of who I was before Casson passed. I feel more courage and more hopeful about the advocacy work I do. I told him I advocate for him to perhaps being one day released. He added value to that for me. I feel more solid in who I am. It kind of affirmed and confirmed for me what I'm doing. It gave me more boldness to speak on behalf of the lifers."[23]

And as she continues to heal and grow she better and better supports a community in dire need of the process of restorative justice, victims and offenders alike.

LEARN MORE

Restorative justice really is being used in schools and neighborhood groups as well as prisons. It can be a powerful way of practicing a different form of justice that honors everyone's humanity or capacity. And it can actually offer more possibility for healing to a victim of a crime than the current system of retributive justice as well as potentially correcting for the racial bias that saturates that system. A great entry point resource on why restorative justice models can be good for schools to adopt, check out the article by the Alliance for Excellent Education, "Five Things Parents Need to Know About School Discipline," written by Kristen Loschert, October 11, 2016, All4Ed.org.

The country of South Africa has an excellent online primer on restorative justice: www.justice.gov.za, search "restorative justice booklet."

The United Nations has an entire e-book that touches on criminal justice and family circles and use with juvenile communities, www.unodc.org, search "criminal justice ebook."

PBS showed a riveting film about people engaged in the work of interrupting violence in Chicago through restorative justice models. The film is called *the Interrupters* and is a great way to glimpse the process of restorative justice. Interrupters. kartemquin.com

---

23 Kevin Simpson, "Denver woman feels the power of restorative justice after son murdered," July 9, 2012.

To find a restorative practices trainer who works with schools or any number of books on creating restorative circles in any number of venues, visit Living Justice Press's website: www.livingjusticepress.org

If you would like to talk with people inclined to being skeptical about the restorative justice model, the article "How Restorative Justice Changed This Colorado Cop's Views on Prison" might be a great resource to share, www.yesmagazine.org.

To imagine a restorative justice circle in your community and what it would entail on a small scale, check out this resource from the Student Peace Alliance on peace circles and the restorative justice model, www.studentpeacealliance.org.

4

The Power of Keeping It Simple:

Humans Deserve Housing

"Housing is a human right; we will not give up the fight!"
POPULAR CHANT DURING OCCUPY WALL STREET

It is hard to argue that housing is not a fundamental human need. Decent, affordable housing should be a basic right for everybody in this country. The reason is simple: without stable shelter, everything else falls apart.
—MATTHEW DESMOND, *EVICTED: POVERTY AND PROFIT IN THE AMERICAN CITY*

When Cheri Honkala says that there are more empty houses in the United States than homeless people, there are policy think tanks and nonprofits like Amnesty International that will back her up on that claim, with estimates running from five homes per homeless family in the wake of the 2008 housing crisis to a possible ratio of six to one.

According to one article describing the neighborhood in 2004, "Kensington [in north Philadelphia] was once a major manufacturing center. In 1903, Mary Harris "Mother" Jones led her famous March of the Mill Children from Kensington to the summer retreat of President Theodore Roosevelt in Oyster Bay, Long Island, to protest child-labor abuses. Today, most of the area's factories are burned-out shells, and the unemployment rate hovers in the teens."[24] Honkala had

---

24 Ron Feemster, "Economic Rights are Human Rights," *Shelterforce Magazine*, National Housing Institute, Issue #135, May/June 2004.

moved there because it was one of the only neighborhoods she, as a single mother, could afford, even though she worried for her children's safety and was quickly frustrated with the lack of children's programming available in the community.

Honkala helped found the Kensington Welfare Rights Union (KWRU) in the early 1990s, when she and five other women created a community center based out of an abandoned welfare office so their children and other children in the community would have activities to do. They were arrested and jailed for six days, and then "we were found not guilty on every count, but we made a strong case for our takeover action—so strong that members of the jury asked us after the trial how they could join our organization and support our cause."[25]

What the Kensington Welfare Rights Union Does

In a piece about KWRU for the Environmental Research Foundation, KWRU's Education Director Willie Baptist said that any effort to organize the poor in the fight against poverty requires five main ingredients:[26]

- First, it requires teams of organizers who are poor and understand the key issues around which poor people will mobilize.
- Second, it requires a base of operations where people can meet to collectively address their needs.
- Third, it requires lines of communication through which information about the struggle can be shared.
- Fourth, it requires mutual support networks (KWRU is aligned with labor unions and student groups, among others).
- Finally, it requires a core group of committed people who can strategize, are politically savvy, and are committed to a long-term struggle.

It is easy to see these ingredients in a story shared by popular evangelical leftist Shane Claiborne about a KWRU

---

25 *Close to Home: Case Studies of Human Rights Work in the United States,* report by the Ford Foundation, 2004. 51.

26 "Kensington Welfare Rights Union," Environmental Research Foundation, http://www.rachel.org.

campaign in 1995:[27] 40 poor families connected to KWRU moved into St. Edward's cathedral, an abandoned Catholic church in North Philadelphia. Somewhat predictably, the diocese gave them 48 hours to evacuate or risk arrest. They said this despite the banner KWRU had hung on the church reading "How can we worship a homeless man on Sunday and ignore one on Monday?" Students from Eastern University showed up, the media showed up, the diocese didn't show up: families stayed in the church for months. The families held a press conference, marched to the mayor's office, told him that he did not understand what it was like to walk in their shoes...and then left their shoes piled in front of his office as an invitation to try to understand their experience. People who saw the coverage offered housing and nudged city agencies to create permanent housing opportunities for families in need. Claiborne eventually moved into the neighborhood and started an intentional community there to continue to support their work. He said, "KWRU taught us the difference between managing poverty and ending it, valuing solidarity over charity. We learned that we are not a voice for the voiceless, for no one is without a voice. We realized many people talk about the poor; but few talk *to* the poor, and even fewer join the voice of the poor. Most of all we learned that love takes risks, gets you in trouble, and sets you free (though you may end up in jail)."

This particular action was not outside the norm for KWRU, which has a history of helping families move into abandoned homes and then navigate the court issues that accompany vagrancy charges. They have helped set up tent cities for the purposes of shelter and for the purposes of pricking the moral conscience of legislators (for example when set up in the rotunda of Philadelphia's city hall). It is a poor people-led movement with partnership from other sectors like labor and the academy. In fact, Willie Baptist was Poverty Scholar in Residence for a number of years at Union Theological Seminary in New York as part of a partnership between a poor people's activist network and the seminary.

---

27 Jill Shook, ed., *Making Housing Happen* (Euguene, OR: Wipf and Stock, 2006) 102.

The Problem They Faced

Few people would dispute the fact that homelessness is a real problem in the United States, along with the burden of housing costs on those facing the greatest barriers. The reasons for these conditions are often blamed on lack of resources. However, as Matthew Desmond states in his book *Evicted*,[28]

> We have the money. We've just made choices about how to spend it. Over the years, lawmakers on both sides of the aisle have restricted housing aid to the poor but expanded it to the affluent in the form of tax benefits for homeowners. Today, housing-related tax expenditures far outpace those for housing assistance. In 2008…federal expenditures for direct housing assistance totaled less than $40.2 billion, but homeowner tax benefits exceeded $171 billion. That number, $171 billion, was equivalent to the 2008 budgets for the Department of Education, the Department of Veterans Affairs, the Department of Homeland Security, the Department of Justice, and the Department of Agriculture combined. Each year, we spend three times what a universal housing voucher program is estimated to cost on homeowner benefits, like the mortgage-interest deduction and the capital-gains exclusion.

> Most federal housing subsidies benefit families with six-figure incomes. If we are going to spend the bulk of our public dollars on the affluent—at least when it comes to housing—we should own up to that decision and stop repeating the politicians' canard about one of the richest countries on the planet being unable to afford doing more. If poverty persists in America, it is not for lack of resources.

This is not a new problem. During his campaign to address the horrific conditions of segregated housing in

28 Matthew Desmond, *Evicted: Poverty and Profit in the American City* (New York: Broadway Books, 2017), 312.

Chicago in 1966, Martin Luther King said, "The Chicago problem is simply a matter of economic exploitation. Every condition exists because someone profits by its existence. The economic exploitation is crystallized in the slum."[29] Homelessness and poverty tear apart families. They create instability in relationships and cause huge emotional stress. They can result in children being separated from parents. They can trigger or exacerbate mental health issues. They decrease school performance. They disrupt people's ability to participate in their community. They increase people's likelihood of ending up in prison and then having even less of a chance of finding decent employment and decent housing.

For any of this to matter, though, the people facing homelessness and poverty must be seen by decision makers as human beings with rights to basic human dignity.

The people building an intentional community in the formerly thriving industrial Kensington neighborhood in Philadelphia faced a fairly simple problem, then: people knew they were struggling. But people with access to resources did not believe they deserved anything other than to struggle.

The people who gave birth to the Kensington Welfare Rights Union faced the problems of low wages, high drug use and crime, homelessness and generational poverty. And more than that, even, they faced the problem of being seen as a problem instead of as human beings.

A New Organizing Framework: Human Rights as a Domestic Issue

In 1996, KWRU staged a fairly unsuccessful protest of federal welfare reform and its severe negative impact on their families; Governor Tom Ridge wouldn't acknowledge them when hundreds of them showed up having marched 140 miles from Philadelphia to Harrisburg. To add insult to injury, their personal possessions were carted off during a bitter cold snap that October. To get out of the cold, a number of them took a public tour of the governor's mansion and noticed the governor's dog basking in the comforts of his elegant home. "What kind of world do we live in that dogs

---

29 Desmond, *Evicted*, 215.

are treated better than humans?" Honkala recalled marchers asking one another.[30]

The Universal Declaration of Human Rights created in 1948 by the United Nations became a bedrock of their work. "We had to base our vision on the essence of being human," Honkala said.

It was an unusual move. Many of the organizers had spent decades being demonized as caricatures of welfare queens and drug runners, justifying politicians' disinvestment in their neighborhoods. Their campaigns had often come in response to the ways they were being dehumanized. And here was a tool people used in global justice work: human rights. Using a human rights framework to discuss their basic needs and how those needs were being ignored by their own government (who had signed the Universal Declaration of Human Rights along with the rest of the UN) would cast a much bigger vision than a local poor people's movement had done in recent memory. And they were doing it while national politicians continued to argue for slashing federal funds for housing and food because, those politicians argued, the recipients of those services were largely undeserving, and in some instances were described as not quite human. As recently as 2014, House Speaker Paul Ryan stated on a morning talk show, "We have got this tailspin of culture, in our inner cities in particular, of men not working and just generations of men not even thinking about working or learning the value and the culture of work, and so there is a real culture problem here that has to be dealt with."[31] Such rhetoric was commonplace during the 1996 Welfare Reform efforts of Democratic President Bill Clinton and the Republican Congress.

KWRU's commitment to poor-people led campaigns with solidarity from other sectors showed up in how they approached restructuring their strategy to effect change in relationship to poor people in their community and around the country. In 1998 they convened a Poor People's Summit

---

30 *Close to Home*, Ford Foundation report, 51.
31 Quoted in Charles M. Blow, "Paul Ryan, Culture and Poverty," *The New York Times* (March 21, 2014).

to bring together people from disparate campaigns around the possibility of human rights as a unifying strategy. "Many of the groups attending the summit—migrant workers, the disabled poor, environmental justice advocates, students and others—quickly realized that human rights principles gave them a road map for a more inclusive movement that could break through barriers that once separated them." Thus was born the Poor People's Economic Human Rights Campaign. The campaign honed in on Articles 23, 25 and 26 of the Universal Declaration of Human Rights as their shared goals:

Article 23. (1) Everyone has the right to work, to free choice of employment, to just and favourable conditions of work and to protection against unemployment.

(2) Everyone, without any discrimination, has the right to equal pay for equal work.

(3) Everyone who works has the right to just and favourable remuneration ensuring for himself and his family an existence worthy of human dignity, and supplemented, if necessary, by other means of social protection.

(4) Everyone has the right to form and to join trade unions for the protection of his interests.

Article 25. (1) Everyone has the right to a standard of living adequate for the health and well-being of himself and of his family, including food, clothing, housing and medical care and necessary social services, and the right to security in the event of unemployment, sickness, disability, widowhood, old age or other lack of livelihood in circumstances beyond his control. (2) Motherhood and childhood are entitled to special care and assistance. All children, whether born in or out of wedlock, shall enjoy the same social protection.

Article 26. (1) Everyone has the right to education. Education shall be free, at least in the elementary and fundamental stages. Elementary education shall be compulsory. Technical and professional education shall be made generally available and higher education shall be equally accessible to all on the basis of merit. (2) Education shall be directed to the full development of the human personality and to the strengthening of respect for human rights and fundamental freedoms. It shall promote understanding, tolerance and friendship among all nations, racial or religious groups, and shall further the activities of the United Nations for the maintenance of peace. (3) Parents have a prior right to choose the kind of education that shall be given to their children.

***

The Poor People's Economic and Human Rights Campaign (PPEHRC) is now a nationwide campaign with partners from coast to coast. Their vision may seem large, but they are aware that poverty is a crisis and abolishing it is the only solution to that crisis. They also know that playing small has not achieved their goals, and their commitment to a large vision always keeps them connected to something bigger than themselves regardless of smaller wins or losses. The federal government's Zero:2012 campaign seeking to end homelessness by the year 2020, starting with chronic homelessness and homelessness among veterans, had some sharp rhetorical hurdles to overcome from the 1996 welfare reform act and earlier Presidential mythmaking about "welfare queens" dating back to the 1980s. It is hard to prove, but the work of KWRU and PPEHRC, among others, may have created enough of a cultural shift to open up the possibility of homeless people being treated by their government as people with rights, even if much of that work is currently being undermined at the same levels of government. Many cities and counties adopted that framework and continue to work towards that goal today.

One Strategy for Collaboration without Co-optation

There is a very specific triumvirate of what PPEHRC does: **"projects of survival"** (food giveaways, housing and land takeovers, community gardens and food distribution), **"movement building"** (marches, national bus tours, and truth commissions to draw attention to human rights violations faced by poor Americans), and **"educationals.**" Educationals are opportunities for poor people who are leaders within the movement to come together with their allies and learn together regularly about skills like door-to-door organizing, growing food, communications strategies when organizing in poor communities, the politics and history of poverty, and more. This is a way to build solidarity among allies and poor people who can co-learn and co-teach on a regular basis to create a foundation for movement-building work.

Those three elements reflect an important strategy: any movement for justice needs to acknowledge people's lived experiences right now and respond to them (like the Black Panther Party of the 70s did with their school lunch programs). Social service programs on their own are not sufficient to create community transformation. And for a movement to thrive, it needs to consistently invest in strengthening the skills of its leaders and also consistently cultivating new leaders. Projects of survival, movement building and educationals create a level of rigor that allows the movement to be sustainable over time, bringing in new people while engaging longtime members. And as they point out in their organizing strategy statement, what do they have to lose?

> We are committed to challenging unjust laws even if it means going to jail. Yes, this is a scary adventure because we are often ignored and they are trying to hide and isolate us. For some of us in this movement, they are beginning to attack. However, we know that we have nothing to lose but the creation of a better world and society to pass onto our children.[32]

The effort of organizing poor people is not an easy task: survival is a full time job. Poverty, as they say, is expensive. And the logistics of poverty are complex. Working multiple jobs, navigating time-consuming social service systems, organizing children's school schedules with work with making sure there is a safe place for them to stay when work

---

32 "Our Strategy," Poor People's Economic and Human Rights Campaign, economichumanrights.org/our-strategy .

hours and school hours don't align, navigating public transit and health care and work...it is shocking that given how time consuming it is to be poor, that any poor people have any energy left for as big a lift as a campaign to eradicate poverty, especially knowing that goal will probably not occur in our lifetime.

What the folks at KWRU found, though, is that a human rights framework has helped poor people in their community to feel seen: their lived experience is not just theirs, but there is language used by people all over the world that speaks to their condition. In that experience, community members have developed a sense of their power and the need for their voice in the work of dismantling poverty. When they are in court defending the fact that they moved into an abandoned home that technically belonged to the city or a bank, they stand with the United Nations and every country that signed the Universal Declaration of Human Rights as they defend themselves. When they decide whether it is worth risking arrest by participating in a tent camp in the city's rotunda to draw attention to homelessness, they do so knowing that they are part of an international movement.

The Poor People's Human and Economic Rights Campaign acknowledges the human dignity and worth of the people who make up the movement. They have made it very simple: housing and work and education are human rights that transcend a profit motive, especially in the richest country in the world. Acknowledge poor people's humanity so that you can respond to their most basic needs and ultimately benefit from the gifts they bring to community when unshackled from poverty and its accompanying burdens.

What Is Being Created Today

Kensington Welfare Rights Union and the Poor People's Economic and Human Rights Campaign have meshed with existing movements and given birth to others, but they have also indirectly influenced many community efforts to create housing justice.

There are many tiny home communities across the country, a number of which are designed specifically to address the homelessness crisis in a given community. The concept of tiny homes is scaled-back size cabins (some as small as 8x8) surrounding a communal space (kitchen/TV room/community room for meetings and parties and other programming), providing people with shelter and privacy as a stepping stone to other permanent housing or sometimes with the goal of building an intentional permanent community. Some emerged out of tent cities that, when city governments got antsy, church groups adopted. Some emerged out of the Occupy Wall Street movement when middle class activists discovered that their protest encampments served as real shelter for others in their community.

Those projects differ in simplicity. They differ in funding structures. They differ in whether they have a nonprofit board structure. There are two things that are similar about all of them: they cost out at a lower rate per unit than federally funded affordable housing does, and if the city has granted them land, it is often far from other community members, due to the stigmatization that homeless people face.

The thing that is reminiscent of KWRU, though, is that a number of those tiny homes projects are resident-run. There is some debate about the effectiveness of that model when resentments can emerge about some people having more power than others, but a community-based decision making process that influences how the community is built and then run connects with the work of KWRU in relationship to *how* housing justice can be lived out. Tiny homes are only one small solution among many to the homelessness crisis in our country, and it is one that only works when land values are such that a city is willing to give the land away for creative use: relative affordability and flexibility are both needed from a city in order to create a community of tiny homes that serve the very diverse homeless populations filling up those homes.

Even among housing justice organizations, the language of housing as a human right has saturated their conversations with policy makers and community members. It is almost conventional wisdom among housing experts to build a

"Housing First" strategy where people are not expected to get their lives together in *order* to get housing but are provided housing *so that* they can get their lives together. Reconstructing who *deserves* housing through a human rights lens has a lot to do with shifting policy perspectives on how to address public policy on homelessness. And that framework aligns with work happening around the country. As Matthew Desmond notes in the book *Evicted*, "Universal housing programs have been successfully implemented all over the developed world. In countries that have such programs, every single family with an income below a certain level who meets basic program requirements has a right to housing assistance."[33] If the United States ever establishes a culture of housing for everyone who wants it, it will be grounded in the notion of housing as a human right, and of homeless people of humans deserving of those basic rights. It is heartbreaking that anyone has to make that case, but it is a gift that KWRU is willing to.

One of the PPEHRC's partners, the Women's Empowerment Agenda Project, had already been in the work of justice for poor people for years when they were invited to the Poor People's Summit in 1998. Ethel Long-Scott of WEAP summed up the importance of that work in the following way: "Having fought a great number of battles in and around welfare rights, we found that we were in large part fighting a defensive fight. That was a fight in which we could only win an occasional battle. The economic human rights movement has been instrumental in helping us and other leaders think outside the box and begin to plan strategically for victory."[34]

LEARN MORE

To learn more about how housing homeless people (including those dealing with addictions or alcoholism or mental health challenges) can be more cost-effective than treating their various conditions without providing housing, read Malcolm Gladwell's article "Million-Dollar Murray" originally printed in the New

---

33 Desmond, *Evicted*, 309.
34 *Close to Home*, Ford Foundation report, 54.

Yorker in 2006 and available at http://gladwell.com/million-dollar-murray/

To learn more about the housing crisis and the connections between poverty and shelter, read Matthew Desmond's acclaimed book *Evicted: Poverty and Profit in the American City,* Crown Publishers, 2016.

To learn more about the role of the U.S. government in creating racial segregation in the American housing market, listen to Professor Richard Rothstein's interview with National Public Radio's Terry Gross on Fresh Air: npr.org, search "Rothstein, government, ghettos."

To learn more about the many models that faith communities have engaged in regarding housing and homelessness issues, from building homes to repurposing old buildings to running policy campaigns, read *Making Housing Happen: Faith-based Affordable Housing Models,* Jill Suzanne Shook, ed. Wipf and Stock Publishers, 2006.

5

The Power of Connection

Communities Overcoming Hate

america:
enter
the gurdwara door is open
our bare feet like cracked glass
our covered heads bulletproof from ego
we turn our backs on bellingham
build our gurdwaras from post traumatic cinder
of bombed birmingham black church
nina simone sings tera bhaana meetha laage[35]
to tune of mississippi goddamn
gunpowder lines noses of children
left behind wailing mummy papa we will never forget you
'the love that forgives' a lullaby
which sears obedient
into a bittering lemon

i stand half mast, america
i grieve for my future son, america
i grieve for all nights, america

i grieve for all nights

—PREETI KAUR, "LETTERS HOME," A POEM DEDICATED
TO THE PEOPLE MURDERED AT THE
OAK CREEK GURDWARA, AUGUST 5, 2012[36]

---

35 A Sikh prayer invoking acceptance of sacrifice. Literally, it means "May I experience Your will as sweet to me."
36 This is an excerpt. More of the text can be found at https://americanturban. com/2012/08/17/letters-home-by-preeti-kaur/.

On the third anniversary of the Oak Creek massacre, Kamal Singh completed a 6k run set up to honor the victims who included his mother and five other Sikh-Americans. As South Asian activist and scholar Deepa Iyer points out, just days after the hate crime by a known white supremacist, then Attorney General Eric Holder said at the memorial service in the now-famous working class suburb just outside of Milwaukee, "We must ask necessary questions of ourselves: What kind of nation do we truly want to have? Will we muster the courage to demand more of those who lead us and, just as importantly, of ourselves? What will we do to prevent that which has brought us here today from occurring in the future?"[37]

At the Sisterhood of Salaam Shalom's third annual conference on December 4, 2016, 500 people came. It is said to have been the largest Muslim-Jewish women's conference to date in the country. As they discussed the incoming President's proposed Muslim registry, Jewish attendee Mahela Morrow-Jones said to her Muslim friend Vaseem Firdous, "If Muslims have to register, we're all going to register."

"You save one life, you save the world. That's what our motto is. That's based on a Hebrew text as well as Quranic text," says Atiya Aftab, co-founder of SOSS.[38]

Why These Different Efforts Were Needed

In the wake of the attacks on the Twin Towers in 2001, some people saw the anger of people in the surge towards war as an understandable reaction to our nation's freedom being violated. People laughed about the U.S. Congress's cafeterias being instructed to serve "freedom fries" instead of French fries when the French would not join America's coalition of the willing in its war in Iraq.

The shadow side of what some people saw as righteous anger was its focus on Muslims, Arab Americans, South Asians, and people who could be mistaken for any of those

---

37 Deepa Iyer, "3 Years After the Sikh Temple Massacre, Hate-Violence Prevention Is Key," ColorLines, August 5, 2015. colorlines.com
38 From a video at facebook.com/MicMedia/videos/1314154241940696

groups. In southern California in the weeks following 9/11, Mexican Americans and Native Americans were attacked, their attackers mistaking them for Muslims, and many Hindu, Sikh, and Muslim people were attacked because of the mistaken assumption that all Brown-skinned people were Muslim and all Muslims were terrorists. The government detained thousands of Muslims and Arab Americans, resulting in no arrests for any terrorist activity.[39]

And yet, with no substantive public expression of regret for racially profiling a group of people of whom no wrong was found, prejudice against Muslims and anyone mistaken for Muslim continued rather than declined. "On the tenth anniversary of 9/11, the DOJ released a report that revealed that hate violence toward people and property (primarily places of worship) had not abated. In the first six years after 9/11, the DOJ investigated more than eight hundred incidences of violence, threats of violence, or arson perpetrated against South Asian, Arab, Hindu, Muslim, and Sikh communities and those perceived to be part of those groups."[40]

When the FBI released their data on hate crimes in 2015 (it takes a long time to compile data, and results generally become available about nine months after the end of the year), they noted that 2015 assaults against Muslims had reached the same level as immediately following 9/11.[41]

The *New York Times* pointed out, in reading the FBI's data, "The rise came even as hate crimes against almost all other groups—including Blacks, Hispanics, Jews, gays and whites—either declined or increased only slightly, his study found. One exception was hate crimes against transgender people, which rose about 40 percent."[42]

---

39 For a very accessible article that also talks about detentions, interference with Muslim charities, and other issues related both to hate crimes and government overreach, read Riad Z. Abdelkarim "American Muslims and 9/11: A Community Looks Back…and to the Future," from the September/October 2002 edition of *Washington Report on Middle East Affairs*: wrmea.org.

40 Deepa Iyer, *We Too Sing America* (New York: The New Press, 2015).

41 Katayoun Kishi, "Anti-Muslim assaults reach 9/11-era levels, FBI data show," Pew Research Center Fact Tank, November 21, 2016, pewresearch.org.

42 Eric Lichtblau, "Hate Crimes Against American Muslims Most Since Post-9/11 Era," *The New York Times*, September 17, 2016, nytimes.com/2016/09/18/us/politics/hate-crimes-american-muslims-rise.html .

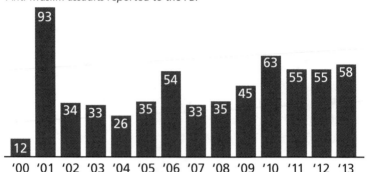

Anti-Muslim assaults at highest level since 2001
Anti-Muslim assaults reported to the FBI

'00 '01 '02 '03 '04 '05 '06 '07 '08 '09 '10 '11 '12 '13
Note: Included simple and aggravated assaults.
Source: Federal Bureau of Investigation

According to the Pew Research Center,

Most Americans say there is "a lot" of discrimination against Muslims in the United States today—roughly six-in-ten U.S. adults (59 percent) said this in a January 2016 Pew Research Center survey. About three-quarters of Americans (76 percent) also said discrimination against Muslims in the U.S. was increasing.

The same survey found that almost half of American adults (49 percent) think at least "some" Muslims in the U.S. are anti-American, including 11 percent who think "most" or "almost all" are anti-American. Another survey from about the same time (December 2015) found that 46 percent of Americans thought Islam was more likely than other religions to encourage violence.[43]

This is a significant part of the hurdle that Arab and South Asian Americans along with Muslims faced: while some people said anti-Muslim violence was on the rise, many Americans also believed that Muslims were anti-American

43 Katayoun Kishi, "Anti-Muslim assaults reach 9/11-era Levels, FBI data show," November 21, 2016, pewforum.org, with links to "Republicans Prefer Blunt Talk about Islamic Extremism, Democrats Favor Caution," Feb. 3, 2016, and "Views of Government's Handling of Terrorism Fall to Post-9/11 Low," December 15, 2015.

and prone to violence, decreasing the likelihood of their willingness to stand up for the community. And as a result, many people mistaken for Muslim would suffer along with innocent and peace-loving Muslims, such as Sikhs whose turbans seem to trigger something in people looking to release their rage. (Anti-Sikh attacks were not tracked as hate crimes by the FBI until 2015, and their numbers are tracked separately from anti-Muslim attacks, making it hard to know exactly how many attacks are due to Islamophobia and how many are due to anti-Sikh or simply white or Christian Supremacist motives.)

This experience of hate crimes is familiar territory for another religious minority in the United States: Jewish people. More than half of hate crimes are race-based, with the majority of those hate crimes being against Black Americans. Of religiously based hate crimes, Jewish people are the most likely to face that form of violence, even with the alarming spike in anti-Muslim violence in the past decade, according to the FBI:[44]

Religiously motivated hate crimes reported in the United States, 1996–2015

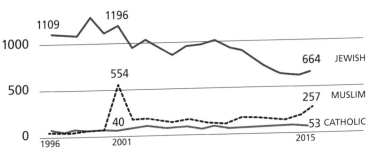

Jewish, Muslim, and Catholic refer to the religions of the victim(s).
Source: Federal Bureau of Investigation Uniform Crime Report

Jewish people also face the assumption that all Jewish people are Israeli and that all Israelis support an anti-Palestinian position, but in addition to that, they face literally thousands of years of attempted dehumanization and even attempted genocide, particularly throughout Christian

44 From washingtonpost.com.

history. This persecution is so deeply embedded within that history that most Christians do not realize that the Holocaust of World War II was only the most recent attempt to exterminate Jewish people, and that the church was at the forefront of many of those attempts.[45] So it is not surprising that the Southern Poverty Law Center notes that of the 892 active hate groups in America, 521 of them include anti-Jewish convictions.[46]

"There's so much hate out there, there's so much distrust. There's so much lack of respect. It's easy to hate someone you don't know, " says Sheryl Olitzky, founder of Sisterhood of Salaam Shalom.[47]

The Tool of Intentional Relationship

After the attack on the gurdwara, it would have been understandable if the Sikh community had sought to disappear: cut off their beards and hair (which they traditionally let grow out for religious reasons), stop wearing turbans, try to blend in as best they could despite their Brown skin.

However, when Deepa Iyer visited with the young Sikhs in the community, she discovered the opposite: Kanwardeep Singh actually began wearing a turban and growing out his hair in order to engage directly with the community *as a Sikh*. "I don't shy away from conversations about my faith," he said. "I have random conversations with people about who I am on purpose, while I'm at the gas station or walking down the street....It is important to learn the stories of others and find a sense of common humanity."[48] Young Sikhs in Oak Creek are engaging outside of the gurdwara, connecting with civic institutions and even aspiring to have a voice to shape the wider community beyond the Sikh community. They reach out to other groups sometimes on the margins: LGBTQ

---

45 For more on this, PLEASE read *Constantine's Sword: The Church and the Jews, A History*, by James Carroll.
46 Feinberg, "These 4 factors trigger anti-Semitic hate crimes in the U.S.," Monkey Cage, *The Washington Post*, December 21, 2016, https://www.washingtonpost.com/news/monkey-cage/wp/2016/12/21/these-4-factors-trigger-anti-semitic-hate-crimes-in-the-u-s/?utm_term=.6e544e46e276.
47 From a video at facebook.com/MicMedia/videos/1314154241940696/
48 Iyer, *We Too Sing America*, chapter 1, loc 781.

organizations and other groups of people of color. They have tapped into leadership development programs for people of color to learn skills but also build deeper relationships, and to transcend the segregated neighborhoods they live in.

And in the process they have had to do some inner reflection: "The liquor stores located in the north side of Milwaukee, where Black people live, are owned mainly by our own people," commented Navi Gill. "And even though we do business there, we keep African Americans at a distance. Why? We have to change this."[49]

When new immigrant communities move to this country, they often build up a support system to take care of each other and help each other navigate this new terrain. That is a critical survival resource for immigrants who arrive here as youth and adults, but it has two limitations: (1) it does not allow immigrants to build up relationships of trust as a community with those around them, and (2) it means that they do not necessarily get to learn about the complex racial landscape of this country and their role in it.

Much of the reason for hate crimes in this country is that people have no relationship with people different from themselves. Hate groups thrive on the division between communities embedded in this nation. They have many opportunities: according to a 2013 study by the Public Religion Research Institute, the average white American's friend circle is 1 percent Black, 1 percent Latino, 1 percent Asian, and 1 percent mixed race.[50] White Americans hear much more *about* communities of color than *from* them. (That same study indicated that people of color have white friends as well as friends from their racial background but may not have as many friends from other communities of color, meaning that they often hear more about each other than from each other as well.)

What is powerful about the work of the Oak Creek young adults, many of whom came here as children or were born here, is that they have enough grounding to do the work that their parents may not have been able to: build relationships

49 Iyer, *We Too Sing America*. Loc 795 .
50 See prri.org/research/poll-race-religion-politics-americans-social-networks .

with non-Sikhs, and recognize their connection to and their impact on other communities on the margins. They are doing the work of prevention: preventing alienation, possibly preventing the irrational hatred that leads to the inexplicable violence they had to endure, and preventing brokenness between them and other communities who have dealt with contempt and hatred for centuries in this country.

They are not alone; there are many groups and movements emerging to reduce uninformed fear and build bridges, like the "Meet a Muslim" video that went viral in 2016 and Muslim people doing their own live versions of Meet a Muslim, making themselves available to go to churches and libraries and town halls and community festivals to share their own experiences and share about their faith and answer questions. In numerous moments of solidarity over the past year, as mosques have been threatened, people of other faiths have shown up to surround the mosque with support and prayer (Hands Around the Mosque events have occurred all over the country), and mosques have invited community members to worship with them, have meals with them, and get to know them and their space. Bay Area Solidarity Summer is a youth program in northern California that brings South Asian youth together to learn organizing skills to advocate for their own community. They also learn about Black-Brown solidarity in this country, paying attention to the ways South Asian Americans have been assimilated into a culture that teaches them to devalue their African American brothers and sisters, and lifting up the untold stories of how South Asians and African Americans have supported each other throughout U.S. history as a model for the future.

***

Another beautiful way this type of relationship building has emerged is through the Sisterhood of Salaam Shalom, originally a group of 12 women in New Jersey that now has local chapters all over the country.

"Women navigate the world through relationships. The relationships that are built by bringing together Muslim and Jewish women, who share so many practices and beliefs, are life-changing and can help put an end to anti-Muslim and anti-Jewish sentiment. We influence family, friends and the general public about our strength in coming together to build bridges and fight hate, negative stereotyping and prejudice. We are changing the world, one Muslim and one Jewish woman at a time!" writes Sheryl Olitzky.[51]

After a visit to Poland in 2010 when Sheryl was struck by what hate had wrought in relationship to her Jewish community, she came back to the U.S. determined to make a contribution to reducing hate. She contacted an imam she knew who introduced her to Atiya Aftab, and the two women invited an additional five Jewish and five Muslim women to meet monthly. They are now a national organization with local chapters all over the country. While they talk about ending hatred one Muslim and one Jewish woman at a time, they actually recognize the power of community in effecting change. Why only women? "Researchers in the field of neuroscience (Tannen 1990, Pease 2001, Benko and Pelster 2013) suggest that women's brains work differently than do the brains of men, providing women with a greater capacity for consensus-building and the ability to have a conversation with one another to negotiate closeness."[52]

As local chapters took off, they chose to focus on *dialogue*, *socialization* and *social action* ("an organized activity to focus on the betterment of others"). According to SOSS board member Amber Khan, the local Kansas City chapter's social action was to step in and provide meals at a local cancer treatment center during Christmas so that the Christian volunteers could spend the holiday with their families, creating another relational bridge in the process. She also said there was something really powerful in the fact that in order to deal with anti-Semitism and Islamophobia, the women needed to confront the "isms" they had internalized about each other in order to be in true relationship with each other, and that has been some of the most powerful work she has witnessed.

---

51 See sosspeace.org/who-we-are/letter-executive-director-2
52 "Building Jewish-Muslim Friendship One Woman at a Time," Sheryl M. Olitzky, January 8, 2015, theinterfaithobserver.org.

What Amber values is that the women of the local chapters "are not professional organizers; they're women who said, 'my community needs healing and I want to be a part of that.'" When white nationalists desecrated mosques, the Jewish community showed up in force, sometimes even sharing worship spaces.

"I think there's more of a sense of urgency," says Aftab at the Sisterhood. "We've heard from people all over the country, even all over the world, saying, 'I need to reach out and do something constructive rather than be affected by this fear in a negative way.'"[53]

What It Looks Like Now

At the third anniversary 6k run in Oak Creek in 2015, Robbie Parker came and spoke. His daughter was one of the 20 children and six teachers killed in Newtown, Connecticut just four months after the hate crime in Oak Creek. According to Deepa, "he connected Newtown's experiences of loss, pain, and psychological trauma with those of the Oak Creek community." That connection was not an abstraction: just after Kamal had lost his mother in Oak Creek, he learned of the Newtown shooting. Within a few week, he got on a plane to New York carrying a banner made by the community: *Sikh Temple of Wisconsin and Oak Creek Stands With You.* They drove to Newtown to deliver it. "Right when we got off the highway, there was a tent. We went there first, and there were thousands of teddy bears and a huge bunch of posters, flowers, and memorabilia for the kids, the police officers, the teachers. I cried for about 20 minutes because I thought it was so powerful. We took the banner inside, but the lady that was in charge there, she recognized me and saw me crying. I told her who I was, and she couldn't believe we came all the way from Oak Creek. It was the most amazing thing I've ever done."[54]

Amber from the SOSS board recently bought a pair of shoes at a SOSS event. They fund the Parents' Circle

53 Jessica Mendoza, "Why Jews are coming to the defense of mosques in America," *Christian Science Monitor,* December 1, 2016. csmonitor.com.
54 Iyer, *We Too Sing America,* loc 831.

through the "Taking Steps in the Path of Peace" project; the shoes were made in Israel and hand stitched with a dove in Palestine. They support people of both communities, and they support a project where people who have lost family to Palestinian-Israeli conflict are entering into relationship with each other across religious lines to know each other as brothers and sisters. One of the leaders, Robi Damelin, lost her son, an Israeli soldier, when he was shot by a Palestinian affiliated with Hamas; her story is one of the stories featured in the film *Beyond Right and Wrong* about reconciliation in the face of violence. Amber got to meet Robi, and said, "What's so powerful is she's creative and looking for ways to create peace. Plenty of people tell her she's breaking the norms. And her response is, 'I didn't say this was easy, but what's the option; more blood? And if you journey with them, you realize their blood is the same as ours.'"

What Else Could Happen Now

In an October 2015 article on the third anniversary of the Oak Creek shooting, Deepa Iyer proposed some ways to move forward proactively, not just reactively in the wake of hate violence. Some might think these proposals are impossible in the current administration, but they are tangible actions to stem the tide of growing violence against racial and religious minorities and they mesh well with the culture shift work that SOSS and the youth from the Oak Creek gurdwara are doing on our behalf and for the soul of our nation and world:[55]

- Instead of being in a defensive posture after the fact— of convening interfaith conversations on the ground, implementing government task forces, investing in security measures to protect congregates, and utilizing weak federal laws to prosecute perpetrators—we must be prepared to confront and eliminate patterns of hate violence before it occurs. Affirmative steps include a federal focus on right-wing extremist groups, whether that means characterizing their activities as

---

55 Deepa Iyer, "3 Years After the Sikh Temple Massacre, Hate-Violence Prevention Is Key," *Color Lines*, August 5, 2015, colorlines.com .

violent extremism or domestic terrorism, conducting threat assessments, and monitoring their tactics and strategies—all of which are activities that the federal government regularly engages in to counter Muslim "radicalization." The White House and Congress must call for and support inter-governmental task forces to respond to the epidemic of hate violence at places of faith, requiring regular reports and setting benchmarks for their progress.

• State lawmakers can pass legislation denouncing hate violence and setting aside funds for rapid-response tools. Educators can design and implement mandatory curricula that teach children to respect and understand the racial and religious diversity in their communities.

• Media outlets can end the use of hypocritical narratives that characterize perpetrators differently when they are people of color or Muslim (usually called "terrorists") as opposed to white perpetrators (usually called "lone white males"). Philanthropic institutions can support participatory research by nonprofits that enables us to better understand the impact of living with the threat of hate violence. Communities of color and faith can continue to make the connections between hate and state violence, both of which are often premised on anti-Black racism, anti-immigrant sentiment and Islamophobia.

To alleviate the current crisis, we will need to be bold in the ways we advocate for a society that supports us all and leaves none of us living in legitimate fear for our safety, including Sikhs, Muslims, Hindus and others mistakenly perceived to be a threat.

And as we seek to create real, bold solutions to the institutional policies and media that perpetuate fear and division in our nation right now, let us take a leaf also (but not only) from our brothers and sisters in Oak Creek and our Sisters of Salaam Shalom and the many others seeking to bridge the divides so that before another attack happens, before another dangerous policy is passed, we will know each other and value each other enough to protect one another.

LEARN MORE

To learn about South Asian and Muslim and Sikh organizations you can reach out to in this political moment, learn more about the following groups:

- AROC (Arab Resource and Organizing Center): http://araborganizing.org/
- CAIR (Council on American Islamic Relations): https://www.cair.com/
- SAALT (South Asian Americans Leading Together): http://saalt.org/
- Muslim Advocates: https://www.muslimadvocates.org/
- Sikhnet: https://www.sikhnet.com/
- Sikh Coalition: https://www.sikhcoalition.org/

Also, do take the time to read *We Too Sing America* by Deepa Iyer. The story of young Sikhs in Oak Creek is only one of many inspiring stories about the next generation in the South Asian community even in a post-9/11 climate.

To learn more about *relationship building across religious lines*, check out:

- Sisterhood of Salaam Shalom: sosspeace.org.
- The Parents' Circle (beginning American chapters now): theparentscircle.com.
- United Religions Initiative: uri.org.
- See the film Fremont, USA and check out additional resources at the Pluralism Project about faith communities coming together in solidarity: pluralism.org/films/fremont-usa.

To better understand the potential pain and disconnect for Muslim Americans doing something like a "Meet a Muslim" event, please take the time to read the *Washington Post* article "Love Thy Neighbor?" by Stephanie McCrummen published July 1 and available by searching http://www.washingtonpost.com. The subtitle of the article is "When a Muslim doctor arrived in a rural Midwestern town, 'it felt right.' But that feeling began to change after the election of Donald Trump." See if your community has an interfaith council. If not, bring together folks yourself! Many councils have started because people from a mosque, synagogue and church decided to share meals together and learn about each other's spiritual lives and cultures.

If you would like to engage in a support system so you are prepared to act in case a mosque or synagogue or church is attacked in your community, here are a couple of resources to bring to your planning meeting with a diverse group of community and faith leaders to create a Safety Plan:

- Protecting Houses of Worship Event Resource Guide: ise.gov/resources/document-library/protecting-houses-worship-event-resource-guide.
- Resources to protect your house of worship: fema.gov/faith-resources.
- Recommended best practices for securing houses of worship, provided by ASIS security: sacramentointerfaith.org, search "ASIS best practices."

Please note: given the value of collaboration emphasized in this book, strongly consider using the above resources only as a supplement to intentional efforts to build solidarity and connection between faith communities. Interfaith groups have created phone trees so that if a faith community is threatened, the appropriate people are notified, the media is contacted to cover the story of interfaith solidarity in the face of hate, and faith communities even create space for people to attend open houses or get tours of facilities to reduce barriers among neighbors. Doing this with interfaith partners creates some additional protection as well as emotional support when a faith community takes such a big risk.

Also, for people of faith, additional preventative work can be done around bullying, which leads to bigger issues among adults: stopbullying.gov, search "faith leaders."

6

The Power of Empowering Community

*Of all our national resources—natural and man-made—
the most important, and the one in terms of which all the
others have to be judged, is human life. The safety, welfare
and happiness of the men, women and children who compose
the American people constitute the only justification of
government. They are the ends for which all our resources…
are merely instruments. The manner of life of our people, the
problems they face, and the hopes and desires they cherish
for improvement in their existence and the advance of their
civilization should be the supreme concern of government.*

—"Our Cities: Their Role in the National Economy,"
written for President Franklin D. Roosevelt as
groundwork for the New Deal[56]

"Tony Hernandez remembers playing as a child on the
vacant lots in the Dudley Street neighborhood of Boston. In
the 1980s, white flight and disinvestment had so devastated
this neighborhood that more than 20 percent of the land—
1,300 lots—lay vacant. Today, Hernandez owns a home on this
land, one of 225 units of permanently affordable housing. His
home is surrounded by parks and gardens, a town common,
community center, charter school, community greenhouse,
and several urban farms. This transformation was led by
residents of the Dudley Street Neighborhood Initiative, who
in the late 1980s established a community land trust to take
democratic ownership of the land and guide development."[57]

---

56 "When Half the Neighborhood Is Missing," Gus Newport; originally published
in *Nonprofit Quarterly,* 178. NOTE: Any additional quotes from Gus Newport
come from a personal interview June 2, 2015, unless otherwise noted.
57 Penn Loh, "How One Boston Neighborhood Stopped Gentrification in Its
Tracks," *YES! Magazine,* January 28, 2015, yesmagazine.org.

So begins one of dozens of articles touting the success of the Dudley Street Neighborhood Initiative (DSNI), a community project almost unique in the United States in that it turned an incredibly poor neighborhood into a path to home ownership and thriving green space and small business ownership for African Americans and immigrants without resulting in the gentrification that so often accompanies "urban renewal" or "neighborhood revitalization" projects.

According to Gus Newport, who ran the Dudley Street Neighborhood Initiative in the late eighties and early nineties, it was the only inner city community not to face one foreclosure during the predatory lending crisis of the early 2000s made famous in the blockbuster film *The Big Short*.

How did this neighborhood move from barely surviving to thriving over the course of three decades?

Why DSNI Came into Being

In 1984, the Dudley Street neighborhood of Boston knew well the challenges of drugs, violence, arson and abandoned lots. "A lot of home owners moved out, torched their homes and waited for the neighborhood to come back," explains Gus. As a result, there were 30 acres of vacant land, 15 of which were owned by the city through tax arrears. Additionally, meat packing companies, car chop shops and others would dump their waste in poor communities of color to save dumping fees, knowing they would not be penalized. The city was getting ready to pursue redevelopment in a new area, much like cities across the country in that era. Each time they engaged in "urban renewal," financially investing in neighborhood improvement, a whole new group of people got displaced. The city seemingly didn't factor in (or perhaps even hoped for) the rental and home ownership cost increases that would accompany the renewal process.

The conditions in the Dudley Street area did not emerge out of nowhere. "White flight," the departure of white middle class people from urban areas, was supported by government programs which created suburbs, benefiting developers and allowing a path to home ownership for the people who were allowed to buy homes in those communities (generally only

White people), sometimes subsidized by the GI Bill after World War II. Simultaneously, even veterans of color who could benefit from the GI Bill had fewer home ownership options available to them due to banks not allowing people of color to purchase homes in many suburban neighborhoods (a practice known as redlining), leaving many renting in urban communities that faced disinvestment by local and regional government. As Gus says, "they created inner city communities without cultural centers or business communities or open spaces, communities without resources or hope, and then blame the people living there for the violence in those communities."

The neighborhood, which 40 years ago had been Irish and Jewish, was now a mixture of African Americans who had arrived during the Great Migration from the South and immigrants from places like Cape Verde and the Dominican Republic and other mostly low-income, mostly Black and Brown immigrants, as well as some older white residents who had not moved out for varying reasons.

People who have never been served by a nonprofit generally assume that nonprofits function in a benevolent and respectful way to the recipients. People may even assume that most nonprofits work collaboratively with people from the neighborhood in creating their vision and living it out. Those people have never heard the expression "nonprofit industrial complex," a term that alludes to how nonprofits, over time, can come to unconsciously focus on perpetuating themselves, often drifting from their core mission and often out of step with both the needs and gifts of the communities they originally intended (and perhaps believe they continue) to serve.

Long before Dudley Street Neighborhood Initiative came into being, there were many nonprofits in the community. In 1984, while the city government envisioned urban renewal of the neighborhood, a downtown Boston-based, well-heeled foundation convened a gathering of the major nonprofits in the area to lay out their own plan for urban renewal of the neighborhood.

As one community resident noted, "You always have people from downtown or somewhere telling you what you need in your neighborhood."[58]

The Tool to Fix Displacement

In his classic article "Why Are We Replacing Furniture When Half the Neighborhood Is Missing?" Gus Newport asks a critical question about the culture of nonprofit and charitable organizations: "Why do some of us serving on nonprofit boards feel that we have enough information at our fingertips without engaging those we seek to help? Isn't it a right of our clients to assist in informing the methods and processes that should be used in upgrading their quality of life?"[59] That question is grounded in what unfolded in the Dudley Street neighborhood effort from 1984 through the present day.

Gus was the director of the Dudley Street Neighborhood Initiative from 1988 to 1992, following his tenure as mayor of Berkeley, California. Prior to that, he was active in the civil rights movement, including extensive work with Malcolm X before Malcolm's murder.

As Gus tells the origin story of Dudley Street Neighborhood Initiative, the large downtown charitable foundation and the neighborhood's nonprofits came together one night in 1984 to lay out their vision, *with no community members involved in the planning or facilitation.*

The meeting itself, though, drew a lot of community people. At one point during the meeting, one of the women from the neighborhood stood up and said, "Everyone's always planning *for* us, no one's ever planning *with* us. We need to stop this right now because we keep getting moved from place to place."

It was a real wake up call to the foundation, who thought that by convening the nonprofits they *had* been working with the community. Their reaction was something along

---

58 Isabelle Anguelovski, *Neighborhood as Refuge: Community Reconstruction, Place Remaking, and Environmental Justice in the City* (Cambridge, MA: MIT Press, 2014), 188.
59 Newport, "When Half the Neighborhood," 180.

the lines of "Wow. We invited all these people to discuss the community *and didn't invite the community*."

The foundation helped to create a way to shape a renewal process based on the express articulated needs of the community, who were seeking a village-like experience (limiting housing heights) with a pathway to home ownership to stabilize their lives. And they supported a community-based collaborative organization *made up of people who really lived in the community rather than just provided services to people in the community*. This organization came to be known as Dudley Street Neighborhood Initiative, and those origins are part of why it has become a national case study: it is shaped *by* the community as well as *for* the community.

***

Two things that set the renewal efforts in the Dudley Street neighborhood apart from other urban renewal projects of the same era were these: (1) <u>community-based participatory research</u>, in which the community was consulted and also helped administer the surveys that determined priorities for improving the neighborhood, and (2) <u>participatory budgeting and policy development</u> (also known as "direct democracy"), in which community members became experts and developed strategy and priorities for how government funding would be spent and nonprofit initiatives would be administered in their community. Additionally, land acquisition from the city government and its placement in a community land trust that guarantees the land cannot be used for the purposes of profiteering made this an almost unique situation. Its core lessons remain important to anyone seeking to engage in the work of "neighborhood improvement" in communities who have historically had little to no agency in shaping priorities in their community.

An illustration of why those things made a difference were residents telling the city they wanted to do the planning process for urban renewal themselves. The city's plan was to build low-income affordable rental housing but not commercial and retail and cultural resources that would create a thriving neighborhood experience instead of just a place to house poor people.

A door-to-door study by a PhD student from nearby MIT along with people in the neighborhood was paired with neighborhood meetings. "When they found the similarity of concerns," says Gus, "otherwise retiring single mothers became empowered." First among those concerns: cleaning up illegal dumping.

Some of the initial projects the community took on were very simple and concrete. Historic churches partnered with their neighbors cleaning up lots, building benches for a park, getting the city to provide dump trucks and start growing wild flowers to replace blight with beauty. Community gardens began to create community and communication and relationship building. According to Isabelle Anguelovski's book *Neighborhood as Refuge*, neighbors became so invested in their community being treated with dignity that they would stand guard at the main entrance to the neighborhood and blockade it when company trucks would try to enter and dump refuse.

Community members also advocated for a business co-op to support local business owners and a human services master plan to increase the effectiveness of the 30 community services agencies serving that neighborhood, a plan the nonprofits resisted fiercely as a threat to their territory. Youth and seniors came together to present skits to the community about what was broken in the neighborhood and the community's power to change it. Parents demanded playgrounds at schools that were not simply concrete.

"What we instilled into the organization was this value," says Gus: "organizing is a necessary part of the work. ALL of us have to be organizers. All of us have to engage the community fairly regularly to let them know what's being accomplished and what's not and why it's not; otherwise rumors fill the void. Every time I went downtown (as director of the Dudley Street Neighborhood Initiative) I would take people with me and we would roleplay beforehand so they felt confident. At these meetings, high level analysts would pull me aside and say 'you're a former mayor—you're letting them call the shots?' And I'd respond, yeah, this is their community; I don't know it all, and they can correct me. That's how you stay grounded in the community and stay on target."

Organizing that was driven by community members resulted in some real success. "In Dudley…activists made creative use of the local (and at times national) political context and benefited from the support of city officials and planners. They often resorted to similar tactics to achieve their objectives, including broad and flexible coalitions and bottom-to-bottom networks encompassing three forms of activism—street activism, technical activism, and funder activism."[60]

Community members, sometimes with little formal education, became experts in how to fund the cleaning of environmental hazards, in how to frame the work so that it resonated with major foundations, in running a campaign to change local policies, in creating a community land trust, and more. Having learned that the community would look different if they took power back from nonprofits who had grown disconnected from the community they had originally intended to serve, community members shaped a major vision with tangible steps (with the help of community organizers). They learned about the history of public policy that had brought them to their current situation, which horrified and angered them but also motivated them to create something new. And over time, the community helped some of the nonprofits rebuild their connection and reorient their mission to be more responsive to the community, resulting in deeper, richer and more effective social services that actually fit both the needs and gifts of the community.

In 1993, almost a decade after DSNI launched, their Human Development Committee helped shape a Declaration of Community Rights that captures the goals of a community development project shaped by the people living in the community[61]:

---

60 Anguelovski, *Neighborhood as Refuge,* 99. In the book, she explains street activism as putting together the existing skills in the neighborhood to create change, technical activism as people in the community learning technical skills to create a nonprofit and create organizational structure as well as learn tangible skills like grantwriting, and funder activism as both organizing funders to engage projects and ultimately getting funders to become activists for the project.
61 DSNI website's historic timeline: dsni.org/dsni-historic-timeline.

We—the youth, adults, seniors of African, Latin American, Caribbean, Native American, Asian and European ancestry—are the Dudley community. Nine years ago, we were Boston's dumping ground and forgotten neighborhood. Today, we are on the rise! We are reclaiming our dignity, rebuilding housing and reknitting the fabric of our communities. Tomorrow, we realize our vision of a vibrant, culturally diverse neighborhood, where everyone is valued for their talents and contribution to the larger community. We, the residents of the Dudley area, dedicate and declare ourselves to the following:

- We have the right to shape the *development of all plans, programs and policies* likely to affect the quality of our lives as neighborhood residents.
- We have the right to quality, affordable *health care* that is both accessible to all neighborhood residents and culturally sensitive.
- We have the right to control the *development* of neighborhood land in ways which insure adequate open space for parks, gardens, tot lots and a range of recreational uses.
- We have the right to live in a hazard-free *environment* that promotes the health and safety of our families.
- We have the right to celebrate the vibrant cultural diversity of the neighborhood through *all artistic forms of expression*.
- We have the right to *education and training* that will encourage our children, youth, adults and elders to meet their maximum potentials.
- We have the right to share in the *jobs* and prosperity created by economic development initiatives in metro-Boston generally, and in the neighborhood specifically.
- We have the right to quality and affordable *housing* in the neighborhood as both tenants and homeowners.
- We have the right to quality and affordable *child care* responsive to the distinct needs of the child and

family as well as available in a home or center-based setting.

- We have the right to safe and accessible *public transportation* serving the neighborhood.
- We have the right to enjoy quality *goods and services*, made available through an active, neighborhood-based commercial district.
- We have the right to enjoy full *spiritual and religious* life in appropriate places of worship.
- We have the right to *safety and security* in our homes and in our neighborhoods.[62]

***

Those values created by the community members who make up Dudley Street Neighborhood Initiative, very different from the values that the charitable foundation and nonprofits who gathered in 1984 would have written for them, continue to guide the priorities, policy work, organizing and social service provision in the Dudley Street neighborhood. They have not achieved every part of the dream, but they continue to own the vision together and continue to grow towards it daily.

Where They Are Now

According to Isabelle Anguelovski in her book *Neighborhood as Refuge*, some of the programs in the Dudley Street neighborhood intentionally bring together multiple needs and gifts to create healing for individuals but also strengthen the community. For example, The Food Project has a greenhouse that helps new residents grow vegetables.

Many of those residents are East African immigrants who are here to leave behind war and conflict. So The Food Project also provides clinical support for people to talk through their trauma. "Contact with nature has been linked to mental health problem prevention and treatment," notes Anguelovski. "Yet places like gardens heal both individual wounds and also collective ones. In Dudley, the greenhouse had a therapeutic benefit for marginalized groups. A few hundred yards away, the Boston Schoolyard initiative rebuilt

---

62 "History," on DSNI website, http://www.dsni.org/dsni-historic-timeline/.

outdoor classrooms and playgrounds to heal residents, soothe relationships within the neighborhood, and strengthen connections between schools and families. The new green spaces are soothing and therapeutic."[63]

Additionally, in a cross-cultural community such as the Dudley Street neighborhood, the gardening spaces can become bridge-building spaces: "When people come into the garden, the one agenda is gardening," explains a staff member of the Boston Natural Areas Network. "So even people who don't speak the same language, I've seen communicate absolutely clearly over squash or tomato. You know, it's a profound community-building process, absolutely profound. Get a group of people to really work well together even if they don't like each other."[64]

In communities across the country, low-income communities that have invested heavily in community redevelopment are watching white, wealthier people move in to benefit from the improvements they made while they are pushed to the next low-income community. DSNI has done an amazing job of resisting "gentrification" through intentional community-based efforts. The organizing principle is sometimes called "right to the city," the belief that the city belongs to the people who live here more than to the people or corporations or governments who own the land. In the earliest days of organizing in the Dudley Street neighborhood, the fight was to keep outsiders from using the neighborhood as a dumping ground. This involved "residents...fighting the stigmas that were associated with their place while restoring a sense of dignity to residents," says Anguelovski in *Neighborhood as Refuge*.[65]

Later they faced the challenge of making the neighborhood both physically and environmentally safe without creating the kind of neighborhood that would make wealthier people want to move in and displace the residents who built up the community in the first place: development without displacement. DSNI got the city to place some of the land in a trust so it cannot be used for profiteering, and they

63 Anguelovski, 145.
64 Anguelovski, 188.
65 Anguelovski, 191.

have bought additional land when their nonprofit could manage over the years to protect the land around them from similar speculation. A large part of this work has been through revisioning how they locally create a democratic process: "Building the type of neighborhood that community members envision cannot occur without asking who makes decisions in the neighborhood, whom they benefit, and which benefits are distributed. Environmental projects thus become a tool for questioning broader political arrangements in the city, empowering residents, and creating new, spontaneous, self-managed, and at times anarchical forms of participation and decision making."[66]

From its beginnings, community organizing has moved the Dudley Street neighborhood forward; key to that, though, was the type of organizing that recognized the *voice* and *power* and *commitment* of people in the neighborhood where dozens of charitable organizations had only seen *people in need* of basic resources. The voice and skills and labor of the community continue to guide its growth and will continue to do so for many years to come.

LEARN MORE

If you want to learn more about the Dudley Street Neighborhood Initiative, there is a very simple five-minute video available on YouTube at https://youtu.be/97mE4f6yuQM. For a deeper dive, Isabelle Anguelovski's book *Neighborhood As Refuge: Community Reconstruction, Place Remaking and Environmental Justice in the City* looks at the successes and challenges of DSNI alongside a similar movement in Barcelona and one in Cuba. The way most people learn about DSNI is from the highly regarded documentary *Holding Ground: The Rebirth of Dudley Street*, made when DSNI was about 12 years old: newday.com/film/holding-ground-rebirth-dudley-street. The same filmmakers made a sequel, *Gaining Ground: Building Community on Dudley Street* for DSNI's 25th anniversary: newday.com/film/gaining-ground-building-community-dudley-street

At the heart of DSNI's success is the community voice, leadership and labor. However, DSNI would have looked VERY

---

66 Anguelovski, 193.

different without a substantive donation of land to start the project off and then the purchasing of additional blighted land to put into a *community land trust*. With a CLT, the land can never be used for profit, assuring that home values will not rise at market rate and creating a pipeline for home ownership. Community land trusts are a great way of protecting land from speculation and providing permanently affordable housing or community space. To learn more about this technical issue, visit the National Community Land Trust Network: cltnetwork.org.

While the people who helped launch DSNI wouldn't necessarily have used the term "Community-Based Participatory Research," that model can help give some insight into how the members of the Dudley Street community self-organized. According to the WK Kellogg Foundation Community Health Scholars Program, CBPR is a "collaborative approach to research that equitably involves all partners in the research process and recognizes the unique strengths that each brings. CBPR begins with a research topic of importance to the community, has the aim of combining knowledge with action and achieving social change to improve health outcomes and eliminate health disparities." Additional information can be found at the Community-Campus Partnerships for Health at depts.washington.edu/ccph/commbas. html, the U.S. Department of Health and Human Services at archive.ahrq.gov/research/cbprrole.htm, and through the excellent policy organization Policy Link at policylink.org/sites/default/files/CBPR.pdf.

A resource that can complement community-based participatory research is "Participatory Budgeting." In an informal way, this is part of how the community in the Dudley Street neighborhood engaged in the city's proposed redevelopment proposal, rejecting it and reorganizing how funding priorities would be created for their community. This process allows community members to directly decide how part of the public budget is spent. To learn more about this model and how it has been used, visit the Participatory Budgeting Project at participatorybudgeting.org.

7

The Power of Truth
(and Reconciliation)

*"They say war is hell, but I say it's the foyer to hell. I say
coming home is hell, and hell ain't got no coordinates."*
—TYLER BOUDREAU, IRAQ WAR VETERAN

*"Today we reap some of the harvest of what we sowed at the
end of a South African famine. And in the celebration and
disappointment that attends such harvest, we know that we
shall have to sow again, and harvest again, over and over, to
sustain our livelihood; to flourish as a community; and for our
generation to know that when we finally go to rest forever, our
progeny will be secure in the knowledge that two simple words
will reign: Never Again!"*
—NELSON MANDELA, ON RECEIVING THE OFFICIAL REPORT
OF THE SOUTH AFRICAN TRUTH AND RECONCILIATION
COMMISSION REPORT, OCTOBER 29, 1998

Today, there are churches and mosques and synagogues
all over the country working to support returning military
men and women dealing with the trauma of what they
participated in or witnessed in combat.

There are scholars looking into the connections between
neuroscience and ritual to provide healing.

There are veterans' groups creating space for the men
and women who fought in battles in Iraq and Afghanistan
and Vietnam to talk about the soul-deep burdens they carry.

The U.S. Department of Veterans' Affairs publicly
acknowledges a struggle veterans face known as "moral

injury," and acknowledge it as distinct from post-traumatic stress disorder (PTSD).[67]

Volunteers of America is about to launch an initiative on moral injury.

***

Before 2010, none of that was true, and moral injury was an almost completely unfamiliar term.

Along with many veterans, Veterans Affairs clinicians and military chaplains who have contributed to more widespread understandings of and work to address moral injury, the Soul Repair Center in Ft. Worth, Texas, deserves credit for the fact that it is now taken so seriously. And the innovative work of Drs. Rita Nakashima Brock and Gabriella Lettini have more than a little to do with that.

Why the Soul Repair Center Began

Few people who have paid attention to the news over the past decade have missed the heartbreaking coverage of the suicide rates and rates of violence among veterans returning from Iraq and Afghanistan. Not all of the violence, self-inflicted or otherwise, was attributable to PTSD, in which a person, when triggered, relives a traumatic moment from their past and cannot escape it. Something else was going on. The need for a Soul Repair Center was very real, but the reasons Brock and Lettini, as feminist theologians and scholars, created it are less obvious until you hear their story.

Brock and Lettini are fairly well known for anti-poverty and anti-war activism. While they both had family connections to people who had served in the military, that wasn't particularly central to their identities or their relationship to one another as colleagues before 2009. How, as people opposed to war, they ended up investing themselves

---

67 According to the National Center for PTSD, there are two potential distinctions: "(1) PTSD is a mental disorder that requires a diagnosis. Moral injury is a dimensional problem - there is no threshold for the presence of moral injury, rather, at a given point in time, a Veteran may have none, or mild to extreme manifestations. (2) Transgression is not necessary for PTSD to develop nor does the PTSD diagnosis sufficiently capture moral injury (shame, self-handicapping, guilt, etc.)," ptsd.va.gov.

in responding to the needs of soldiers was in some ways a matter of chance.

Lettini was living downstairs from some filmmakers who lent her a copy of the 2008 film they had just made, *Soldiers of Conscience*, about soldiers wrestling with issues of conscience in being ordered to redeploy to the Iraq war, including those who returned to war. Four wound up not redeploying, and though all four applied for Conscientious Objector status, only two received it. The other two went to prison rather than redeploy. Lettini was so moved by the film she discussed it with Brock, who saw it in New York at a Tribeca premiere.

"My experience of watching the documentary made me realize how I had been unconcerned with people in the military and that was strange because people I love have served," noted Lettini; "emotionally and in my activism, I had real concern for the civilians in Afghanistan and Iraq but had really removed myself from the soldiers." Lettini realized that her lack of concern for the soldiers was inconsistent with how she functioned as an academic and an activist: in those spheres, she listened to people affected by injustice. She was so upset with the military, though, that she hadn't thought to listen to the soldiers.

Brock, who grew up in a military family, had already done some theological reflection about the damage war does to those who serve in the military as well as to the civilians who suffer through battles and wars. She had written about it with another colleague, Rebecca Parker, in their book *Proverbs of Ashes*. But she also sensed anew a conversation that people weren't having with each other.

There had been some media coverage of men and women applying for Conscientious Objector status during this war. For people who enlist in an all-volunteer the military, this process is complex because CO applicants have to prove they have had a major change of mind and heart and now oppose "war in any form." This means people who want to serve their country but object to a particular war as illegal or unjust must deploy, regardless of their moral objections. (In 1991, 2,500 men and women refused to serve in the Gulf

War on the grounds of conscience, and 111 were eventually granted CO status. During the Iraq and Afghanistan wars at the beginning of the 21st century, far fewer people applied for CO status, but desertions increased significantly during that era.)[68]

The question the film inspired was how to foster the conversation that the country needed, a conversation that was more complex than just "are you for it or against it?"

One Tool the Soul Repair Movement Used

Brock has been known to say, "If you want to resolve a conflict between two opposing sides, make sure there are three or four sides in the room." The great debate regarding the U.S. military tends to be pro-war or anti-war. There are nuances, but it is generally treated as a two-sided debate rather than a multifaceted conversation.

Lettini had used a model called a Truth Commission in her work with the Poverty Initiative at Union Theological Seminary in New York before moving to Berkeley, California, where she and Brock met. The most famous Truth Commission is the Truth and Reconciliation Commission in South Africa, which allowed victims of apartheid to share their stories and have their experiences honored, and offered amnesty to perpetrators of violence in exchange for telling the truth, all for the sake of a post-apartheid South Africa being able to move forward without the weight of apartheid on their shoulders.

Brock, when she was director of a fellowship program for professional women at Harvard, had come to know a member of the South African Commission, Pumla Gobodo Madhikizela, who received a fellowship to write about her experience within months of the commission finishing its work. She had also had extensive conversations in 2006 about how commissions work with her friend Pat Clark, who had served on the 2004 Greensboro Truth and Reconciliation Commission, regarding the Nov. 3, 1979 Klan murder of five anti-Klan demonstrators.

---

68 From the website for the film *Soldiers of Conscience*, "Background: Soldiers at War," pbs.org.

Lettini had co-facilitated a number of Poverty Truth Commissions modeled on a variation of what happened in South Africa, and grassroots truth commissions happening around the world. It was just one tool of many they would use in moving forward their work around what they would eventually call moral injury, but it was an incredibly powerful tool. This tool, coincidentally, was one she had used at Union Theological Seminary when she got to work with the Poor People's Economic and Human Right's Campaign.

In the poverty truth commissions, there were no experts, no nonprofits; the testifiers were poor people speaking about their experiences and how they came to do their own organizing. That is not so unusual, but the people who were used to being treated as experts (policy makers and directors of think tanks and nonprofits) were designated as commissioners, officially in a listening role. Some people used to being the experts initially resisted this role but came to find it powerful. After the public testimony, commissioners and testifiers would think together about how to work together to create solutions to the problems named. Over time they had learned to include accountability teams to guarantee action after the event ended, and action steps were concrete things that the people who recommended them could be involved with.

The Truth Commission on Conscience in War was no small undertaking. A producer from Luna Productions, Ian Slattery, Lettini, and Brock spent two years planning it and raised thousands of dollars to fund it. They invited organizations from across the spectrum to financially invest in the project in exchange for a seat on the commission. They ended up with 75 co-sponsors, ranging from anti-war organizations to veterans organizations, with a wide range of understandings of war, the role of the military, and the role of the U.S. abroad.

Brock and Lettini taught a seminar class on truth commissions for graduate students across the U.S., and 11 of the 12 students served as commissioners, with the 12th offering testimony as an Iraq veteran. The class, in preparation, was able to interview Rev. Peter Storey, who had been appointed by President Mandela to organize the Truth and Reconciliation Commission in South Africa; he talked with them about what it achieved and the things he thought they should have done or done differently. Storey, whom Brock had met in 1993 as he was organizing the Commission, had offered his help to Brock upon seeing an article about Selective Conscientious Objector status; his own son had risked time in prison for refusing to serve in an apartheid military. Students also heard from Ms. Pat Clarke about what it was like to be a commissioner of color on the 2004 Greensboro Truth Commission.

The testimonies for the Truth Commission on Selective Conscientious Objector Status were selected to be diverse, according to Brock: "For a truth commission to work, it cannot be set up as a bunch of political set pieces. The way you can disrupt that is people bringing testimony from a variety of complex positions on an issue, not people who are committed ideologues on an issue but people who are willing to make themselves vulnerable, not to argue but to speak about their own struggles and suffering."

They also spent time preparing the testifiers. "We worked hard to prepare people for the testimony; it can be unethical in such emotionally laden topics, if the person hasn't processed and integrated their experience enough to be on top of the story," noted Brock. "They can become too emotionally exposed and feel like they've been stripped naked in front of a group of people. People mistake that raw emotional exposure for authenticity but I believe it is unkind both to the person exposed and an audience that is put in the role of taking care of or worrying about the speaker, rather than respecting him or her. Remembering can be painful, but if you're harming the person by asking them to tell it, it's not good. If you ask them to tell the story in private multiple times, that's how they get control of it. When done with a lot of preparation and care, sharing the story can be transformative."

When the Truth Commission on Conscience in War finally occurred on March 21, 2010, testifiers included veterans, a Gold Star mother, a VA psychiatrist, an expert on conscientious objection, Muslim and Jewish and Christian leaders, and a former war correspondent. Some veterans were proud of their service; others struggled with it. Five hundred members of the public attended the commission hearing.

One element that created a powerful experience, both Lettini and Brock noted, was the ritual that was embedded in the process. The Commission facilitator, said Brock, explained that "the people who were testifying were speaking from the heart. Our job was not to judge but to take them into our heart."

They lit two candles to create a liminal space: white for death and grief and green for life and hope. They made sure the testifiers were emotionally supported. They did not include Q&A sessions, but let the testimonies speak for themselves. After the closing, the candles were put out.

"If I were doing it in a local community," Brock added, "I would make it longer and would have the second half where people talked together in cross-pollinating ways and were asked to come up with consensus around next steps."

The 125 commissioners and testifiers had all received materials to read before gathering the next day in private. They were tasked with determining achievable goals that they themselves would commit to moving forward. Brock shared an illustration of how powerful that experience was in creating new channels of communication: "During the speak-out, the head of the Mennonite Central Committee, who was one of the commissioners, said, 'I think the pacifists need to repent. I have been to a lot of these events with my just war friends and we're asked to argue with each other. I've never been asked to work with just war people. What I realized is we pacifists let the federal government decide who pacifists are. My just war brothers and sisters and we agree on 95 percent of things and argue about the last 5 percent. We need selective Conscientious Objector status, and I can work with them on that.'"

By the end of the day that incredibly diverse group had put forward the following recommendations:[69]

---

69 "Truth Commission on Conscience and War: Why we need selective conscientious objection," *Daily Kos*, October 25, 2010. https://www.dailykos.com/story/2010/10/25/913576/-

To Our Nation's Leaders Revision of current U.S. military regulations governing Conscientious Objection to assure greater protection for religious freedom and moral conscience in war through the right to object to a particular war.

To Religious and Community Leaders Education of our larger communities about criteria governing the moral conduct of war, about the needs of veterans and their families, including healing moral injury, and about the importance of moral conscience in war.

To Our Communities Education about and support services to address moral injury and other needs of those serving in the U.S. military and veterans of military service and their families.

***

While the commission continues to wait for a change in Congressional leadership that would allow a conversation about the first point, the second was first implemented by Lettini and Brock in their 2012 book with Beacon Press, *Soul Repair: Recovering from Moral Injury After War*. In addition, the Soul Repair Center was among the most substantive actions regarding the second and third points.

And here is where this notion of a truth commission is relevant to anyone seeking to address a major issue of conflict in a community: "I think one very interesting thing that happened is this," notes Lettini:

> We brought together people who stand in very different places in relation to the military and to war. I remember facilitating some moments and having to be firm that we were not there to make statements about the military; we had to create a context where there was enough respect that we could really work together and recognize the common concerns so we could address them. The situation had been heated because after so much apathy, finally people were mobilizing against these particular wars. But the

people we brought together and who kept working together were people who didn't like to work together: pacifists, former military that were now pacifists, some vets who had criticisms but were not anti-military. This forced us to change the spirit of our engagement. Sometimes groups would say "why don't we make a statement against the war" or "why don't we write something to the military" but as a group we needed to try to really take the ideas of everyone to the table to be more effective. This allowed difference to be there but use it to be creative.

That spirit carried from the Commission to other places we had the conversation. Part of the work was we also presented every year to the American Academy of Religion, so there started to be more conversation. And pacifist feminists began to engage womanists who had kept it private that they were former military or had family in the military; there was a coming together across these divides because we didn't jump to name calling. The building of relationships because you stay in conversation and knowing you're different but you keep working together created a context for these conversations to continue through the Soul Repair Center and through AAR and in many other places.

And here's the key part: we intentionally came together across major difference not to convince each other but to be effective around common issues. And by doing that, people would have the conversations, and a lot of transformation happened because of that culture. People moved because the conversation didn't start with us trying to persuade each other… and therefore people were persuaded.

At the beginning of the Truth Commission, the honorary host, Col. (Chaplain) Herman Keizer, Jr., a Vietnam War veteran, had talked about how violating one's conscience was a form of moral suicide. In reflecting on what worked in the Truth Commission model, Brock noted, "we had clear common ground as starting places. We benefited from people who cared about veterans so they could listen to ones whose views were not theirs, and they cared about people's consciences being honored."

Where They Are Now

The Soul Repair Center has trained dozens of faith communities to do the work of talking about moral injury and creating a welcoming environment for veterans wrestling with that issue. They have done work to help the general public understand both the individual and social dimensions of moral injury and its distinctions from PTSD. They have helped communities learn how to support veterans dealing with moral injury, and they have trained clinicians and military chaplains about it. Over time, the institutions designed to support our returning military will be able to provide support for the WHOLE person, the physical, psychological *and* spiritual person.

Community is being built because of this opportunity for people to name their experiences, to finally have language for the things they were encouraged simply to suppress. "It opened conversations that were not happening," says Lettini. "Veterans' communities are having conversations about spiritual issues now that they have the terminology, allowing people to really talk about their experience. Religious leaders are talking about caring for the whole person; military chaplains and anti-war clergy are finding common ground out of a shared compassion."

Brock and Lettini have also experienced this work around moral injury showing up beyond the military community. Lettini has found it to be meaningful in conversations with activists in order to go past rudimentary conversations about burnout and get to issues of where people are carrying harm around with them in the midst of their work. Brock recently received a call from the police department in Perth, Australia, because they recognize that police carry moral injury with them simply because of all they have to witness and handle on a daily basis, even in a city like Perth where police are not armed and rarely involved with issues of police brutality.

But there's another element to the work around soul repair that needs to be recognized in order to do justice to the veterans, something that the veterans Brock and Lettini interviewed for the book *Soul Repair* knew intimately: "Moral injury," notes Lettini, referencing her learning from those interviews, "is not just about the veterans; it's about the whole society. One of the things that upsets the veterans we work with is that society doesn't acknowledge that. Our lack of willingness to acknowledge the damage we caused as a society is actually reinjuring to the veterans. We live in a culture that relies on the profits from war. Unless the whole society takes on the burden and tries to make repairs, the soldiers cannot take on the process of healing and neither can our society. The situation of injustice is what creates the trauma of moral injury."

Too often, the burdens that returning military face are medicalized and organized on a paternalistic dependency model. The work around moral injury challenges that individualistic approach and a long secular tradition of regarding guilt, shame, and remorse as neuroses to be overcome. We do the people who serve in the military a disservice if we regard moral injury as a disorder and only take it as far as caring for the well-being of each veteran. It requires that we talk about who we are as a society and what costs we are willing to inflict on others to maintain our society as it currently exists with war.

The good news is that many veterans are willing to be part of shaping us into a society that doesn't cause people in combat to do things that violate their core self-identity as spiritual beings, and into a society where the people risking their lives can determine whether a cause is worthy of giving their life for. "At the center of this conversation," says Lettini, "are people who both perpetrated and were victims of war. That opened my eyes in a whole new way; I didn't really want to see the complexity of who the soldiers were. They are agents of social transformation; that is the hope. It can be that the people most directly involved can be the ones who help us to transform it, even in the military."

LEARN MORE

To understand more deeply the nuances of moral injury, read *Soul Repair: Recovering from Moral Injury after War,* Rita Nakashima Brock and Gabriella Lettini, Beacon Press, 2012. You can also visit brite.edu/programs/soul-repair to learn more about how you can be trained directly in soul repair work to bring back to your community.

To hear the stories from returned soldiers about the difference between PTSD and moral injury, read the powerful storytelling of David Wood in *What Have We Done: The Moral Injury of Our Longest War,* Little, Brown and Company, 2016.

***

If you're interested in thinking about the societal shifts that may have influenced our current military policies in ways that remove average Americans from a direct relationship to people in our military (and to the unsavory things done in our name), consider reading *Drift: The Unmooring of American Military Power,* Rachel Maddow, Broadway Books, 2013.

If you are interested in learning more about truth commissions, Brock made an important point about their process in distinction from the South African process: "We were not a truth and reconciliation commission. They had state authority. They could grant amnesty to perpetrators. They had three committees: screen and review (what would go before commission), determining which testimonies would be granted amnesty, symbolic recompense for loss. For example, a teacher who loved to sing was killed; they made one of his songs the national anthem. Some who were involved in the South African TRC felt the reconciliation piece was naïve, that the truth commission was a success if it was able to prevent a civil war, and reconciliation could not be achieved so easily."

Bearing that in mind, a classic text on the South African Truth and Reconciliation Commission is Bishop Desmond Tutu's *No Future Without Forgiveness,* Image Press, 1999. Canada's TRC on the treatment of indigenous peoples has also been written about with a specific eye to the role of art (in parallel with Lettini and Brock's reflections on the importance of ritual in their own commission); that book is *Arts of Engagement: Taking Aesthetic Action In And Beyond the Truth and Reconciliation Commission of Canada,* Wilfrid Laurier University Press, 2016. A more wide-reaching text that covers 40 different truth commissions following atrocities is the book *Unspeakable Truths: Transitional Justice and the Challenge of Truth Commissions, 2nd ed.,* Priscilla B Hayner, Routledge Press, 2010.

Because the truth commission model can help a community delve into complex issues in meaningful, bridge-building ways, it is worth looking at an active truth commission related to an issue true to most communities: poverty. Scotland has a Poverty Truth Commission whose work might offer wisdom in thinking through how to create something on a local scale. Information can be found at FaithInCommunityScotland.org/poverty-truth-commission. The Mississippi Truth Project also offers these questions to help think through how a local truth commission might look: MississippiTruth.org/documents/ten-questions.pdf

8

The Power of Blooming Where You're Planted

"We abuse land because we regard it as a commodity belonging to us. When we see land as a community to which we belong, we may begin to use it with love and respect."
—ALDO LEOPOLD

"The most radical thing I ever did was to stay put."
—GRACE LEE BOGGS

Community gardens played an important role in the Dudley Street Neighborhood Initiative, but community gardens and environmental initiatives have begun to play a key role as the starting place in a number of community-driven transformation initiatives all across the United States (and across the globe) for countless reasons.

In Del Norte County, two grocery stores serve the 28,000 people living on 1,000 square miles on the border of Oregon. The Tolowa Dee-ni' native people who live there have had the skills of growing food taken away from them over generations of colonization and in many instances removal from their indigenous land, a reality for many Native Americans across the country, separating them from the land that best supported their local foods. Food insecurity is a reality for high percentages of the population (75 percent food insecurity in the Navajo Nation in Arizona/New Mexico/Utah, where 10 grocery stores cover a territory the size of West Virginia). With few people spread out across large expanses of land, profit-driven grocery stores are not likely to step in to solve the problem. In 2015, the Tolowa Dee-ni' received a USDA grant to plant "food forests" and community gardens. They are now growing vegetables, fruits and squash that go into hot lunches for the elders and to the community's Head Start program. Residents are learning beekeeping and canning for the sake of greater self-reliance and community sustainability. At a time when "Native Americans are twice as likely as white people to lack access to safe, healthy foods—ultimately leading to obesity and diabetes"—the gift of community gardening could literally be saving a nation's collective life.[70]

The Urban Community Garden

In the Bronx, concentrations of industrial waste in the poorest parts of New York City meant people believed that community could only exist as a dumping ground and as housing for the people who could not afford to live anywhere other than a dumping ground. "Sustainable South Bronx," a nonprofit founded by lifelong resident Majora Carter, fought that framing of her community. She had watched the decline in health and economic possibilities in her neighborhood, and as she tells it in her now-famous TED Talk, one day her dog taught her there was more to her community than poverty and pollution: there was a waterfront. There was land hungry to be healed. And there were jobs to be created from the healing of that land—good paying jobs that low-income people could do.

> Our small part of New York City already handled more than 40 percent of the entire city's commercial waste: a sewage treatment pelletizing plant, a sewage sludge plant, four power plants, the world's largest food-distribution center, as well as other industries that bring more than 60,000 diesel truck trips to the area each week. The area also has one of the lowest ratios of parks to people in the city....I'd lived in this area all my life, and you could not get to the river, because of all the lovely facilities that I mentioned earlier. Then, while jogging with my dog

---

70 Amy McDermott, "Growing change: Homegrown food is one safety net in a less stable world for Native Americans," February 18, 2017, Salon.com.

one morning, she pulled me into what I thought was just another illegal dump. There were weeds and piles of garbage and other stuff that I won't mention here, but she kept dragging me, and lo and behold, at the end of that lot was the river. I knew that this forgotten little street-end, abandoned like the dog that brought me there, was worth saving. And I knew it would grow to become the proud beginnings of the community-led revitalization of the new South Bronx.[71]

Inherent in her vision was this: "You don't have to move out of your neighborhood to live in a better one."[72]

And possibly most famously, Asian American civil rights shero Grace Lee Boggs spent the last part of her 100 years on earth investing herself in building community around community gardens in her beloved Detroit, Michigan.

Boggs saw her deeply local work of building the Beloved Community around multigenerational gardening efforts as part of a larger movement, as she shared with Bill Moyers in 2007:

> **GRACE LEE BOGGS:** I see the signs in the various small groups that are emerging all over the place to try and regain our humanity in very practical ways. For example in Milwaukee, Wisconsin, Will Allen, who is a former basketball player has purchased two and a half acres of land, with five greenhouses on it, and he is beginning to grow food, healthy food for his community. And communities are growing up around that idea. I mean, that's a huge change in the way that we think of the city. I mean, the things we have to restore are so elemental. Not just food, and not just healthy food, but a different way of relating to time and history and to the earth.
>
> **BILL MOYERS:** And a garden does that for you?

---

71 Majora Carter, "Greening the ghetto," TED speech, Feb 2006, ted.com.
72 Joanna Gangi, "You Don't Have to Move Out of Your Neighborhood to Live in a Better One," May 11, 2011, *YES! Magazine,* yesmagazine.org.

GRACE LEE BOGGS: Yes. A garden does all sorts of things. It helps young people to relate to the Earth in a different way. It helps them to relate to their elders in a different way. It helps them to think of time in a different way.[73]

Something important about the way Boggs cast that vision, as deeply local but connected to a broader movement to find basic human dignity through community gardens, was captured in an article she co-authored in YES! Magazine in 2011:[74]

When I think of this incredible movement that is already in motion, I feel our connection to women in a village in India who sparked the Chipko movement by hugging the trees to keep them from being cut down by private contractors. I also feel our kinship with the Zapatistas in Chiapas, who announced to the world on January 1, 1994, that their development was going to be grounded in their own culture and not stunted by NAFTA's free market. And I think about how Detroiters can draw inspiration from these global struggles and how—just as we were in the ages of the CIO unions and the Motown sound—our city can also serve as a beacon of Hope.

Grace Lee Boggs is certainly a legend in some circles, but if she is an unfamiliar name, it is probably because she chose to focus her energies into her city of Detroit for much of her adult life right up until the day she died in 2015 at the age of 100. She and her husband James, an auto worker and activist in the Black Power movement, hosted Malcolm X on his visits to Detroit and she unsuccessfully lobbied him to run for Senate in 1964. They chose the term rebellion rather than riot for what happened in Detroit in 1967 because young people were standing up righteously against a state-sanctioned militarized police force they saw terrorizing their community.

---

73 Bill Moyers interview with Grace Lee Boggs, June 15, 2007, pbs.org.
74 Grace Lee Boggs and Scott Kurashige, "Planting Seeds of Hope: How Sustainable Activism Transformed Detroit," June 16, 2011, yesmagazine.org.

Grace Lee Boggs was not a sweet little old Chinese lady who liked to putter in her garden. To her, gardens could create a different form of revolution—because she did see a need for revolution in her beloved Motor City, which would never again know the economic prosperity (or accompanying environmental damage) of Detroit in its most economically vibrant days. As her colleague Richard Feldman, a former auto worker and labor activist notes, "Why Detroit is where it's at is because this all started in 1980. We've had 30 years of living with what people think is a global economic crisis. And folks—enough folks have known that sort of protest politics or expecting the government or the corporations to come back—it's an absurd thought."[75] In other words, these longtime Detroit residents knew that the way forward was not to try to go backward.

In 1991, Boggs and other Detroit locals began a program called Detroit Summer. They borrowed from the best of their learnings from the civil rights movement about activating young people to effect positive change. The summers involved education, organizing training, visioning, building and rehabbing and gardening. As Boggs pointed out, "many adults had come to shun, fear, and ultimately blame [community youth] for so many ills," but Detroit Summer created a venue for the same youth to become part of the solution.

The people who organized Detroit Summer for almost 20 years (variations and evolutions of it continue today through the Boggs Center to Nurture Community Leadership) intended to create something different from the organizations they had seen or participated in up to that point. The two options already widely available were either traditional organizing groups mobilizing youth to protest or large nonprofits seeking corporate and government funding to provide job opportunities and services. The folks dreaming up Detroit Summer believed there could be something more transformative in this moment in Detroit's history. "[O]ur hope was that Detroit Summer would bring about

---

75 Transcript from "Grace Lee Boggs: A Century in the World," *On Being with Krista Tippett*, August 27, 2015, onbeing.org.

a new vision and model of community activism—one that was particularly responsive to the new challenges posed by the conditions of life and struggle in the postindustrial city. We did not feel this could be accomplished if control of our activities was ceded to the dictates of government or the private sector, even though this meant that we would be working on a small scale. However, by working on this scale, we could pay much closer and greater attention to the relationships we were building among ourselves and with communities in Detroit and beyond."[76]

The fruits of that vision are manifold: 1,600 urban gardens in Detroit feeding people, uniting people, and providing local produce to local businesses and restaurants in sustainable ways. Feedom Freedom Growers was founded by Curtis and Myrtle Thompson. Ms. Thompson explains it this simply: "We had a lot of space, we had a need, and the two just went together, especially coming from [Mr. Thompson's] background of activism and building community. Even I wasn't familiar with some of the things that we were growing, but it was just great to grow. So we learned how to prepare those things through the help of a chef and to start to have conversations about why we need to eat better, why we need to eat more nutritionally rich and dense food."[77] She noted that various vegetables draw people to the garden and recipes and cultures get exchanged in the process. She also noted that they've explained to the children who work in the garden that while they can't actually grow pizza, they can definitely grow the ingredients for pizza.

Mr. Thompson adds, "One thing that I think we're going to have to pay more attention to is what food sovereignty is or food security is. I mean, along with growing food, we're growing culture, we're growing community because we're growing structure, we're growing ideology, we're growing a lot of things to make sure that our existence is no longer threatened because of us being marginalized in a system that's killing us and we ain't got no say-so in our existence or how we live as human beings. So developing

---

76 Boggs and Kurashige, yesmagazine.org/people-power/planting-seeds-of-hope .
77 *On Being* interview, Aug. 27, 2015, onbeing.org.

consciousness, I think, is very important. It's just not a warm and fuzzy garden, you know. We're not just growing food, we're becoming part of this process of existence in the whole ecology system that exists not just in the garden, but has existed since the beginning."

Establishing Model Values

In Detroit, and particularly in the network of people connected to the Boggs Center, gardens have in some cases been the beginning of work that has expanded into other issues like employment and medical care and spiritual healing. Gloria Lowe, a brain trauma survivor from her time working with Ford Motor Company, established a program called "We Want Green, Too," a green construction program for disabled war veterans that emerged from a conversation with one of the leaders connected to the Boggs Center. When offering a tour of her home rehabbed by veterans with traumatic brain injury, she explained, "we started this relationship where their whole thing was about the garden and my thing was about houses and how we work with folks in community and try and help them to rehab their souls as well as this place." She works with young men and veterans (some of whom are homeless) who relearn skills by instinct and also rehab existing homes in Detroit which have fallen into disrepair, developing skills that allow them to reenter the job market and also reconnect to their sense of self-worth which was stripped from them during war or after brain injury or for countless other reasons.

"We Want Green, Too" is one of many community-based efforts that have emerged from a small but revolutionary vision in a blighted city with a rapidly declining population. Another project that has emerged is the Boggs School, which seeks to create a more interactive educational environment for the children and youth growing up in Detroit.

Detroit is not the only place this is happening. In addition to the stories from the Tolowa Dee-ni' nation, the Bronx, and Boggs's story from Milwaukee, there is a remarkable project in Oakland called Planting Justice. One of their slogans is "Fresh veggies. Good jobs. A safer, healthier neighborhood."

Much like the work in Detroit, Planting Justice is one of many networks addressing food sustainability and dealing with the other crises of the Bay Area. In particular, Planting Justice recognizes the intersections of the environment, fair wage work and mass incarceration. And their food revolution, like that of the people connected to Detroit Summer, is local. They have a farm in (until recently) beleaguered east Oakland; they run a holistic reentry program so people in prison can learn skills and values that prepare them to be part of the landscaping crew of Planting Justice but also to be part of the movement for eco-justice, worker justice, and prison reform that are essential to healing the community of Oakland. Gardens can sustain more than plants; across the country and around the world, gardens are sustaining a new and ancient way of being community in the face of the failures of other institutions to promote the thriving of the most marginal in our society.

As mentioned before, Grace Lee Boggs was an unapologetic revolutionary her whole life. She believed deeply that this country and this world were designed to serve for the benefit of a few at the cost of many. Her way of fighting that injustice evolved over the course of her life, so that she eventually embraced the nonviolent strategy and spiritual convictions of Martin Luther King Jr., but possibly even more importantly, she began to see revolution less as taking on an unjust government and corrupt corporations and more about building Dr. King's vision of Beloved Community right in one's backyard:[78]

> Living at the margins of the postindustrial capitalist order, we in Detroit are faced with a stark choice of how to devote ourselves to struggle. Should we strain to squeeze the last drops of life out of a failing, deteriorating, and unjust system? Or should we instead devote our creative and collective energies toward envisioning and building a radically different form of living?

---

78 Boggs and Kurashige, yesmagazine.org/people-power/planting-seeds-of-hope .

That is what revolutions are about. They are about creating a new society in the places and spaces left vacant by the disintegration of the old; about evolving to a higher Humanity, not higher buildings; about Love of one another and of the Earth, not Hate; about Hope, not Despair; about saying YES to Life and NO to War; about becoming the change we want to see in the world.

The Boggs School is a powerful illustration of building Beloved Community in one's own backyard: teachers create an environment where children are learning by working in the community—in gardens, in community building projects, in literacy programs—and where they are learning a bigger history of their community than the city's (some would say intentionally) crumbling schools would ever offer. *The mission of the Boggs School is to nurture creative, critical thinkers who contribute to the well-being of their communities.* The school has adopted a model called "place-based education" that, according to their website, "immerses students in local heritage, cultures, landscapes, opportunities and experiences, using these as a foundation for the study of language arts, mathematics, social studies, science and other subjects across the curriculum. PBE emphasizes learning through participation in service projects for the school and local community." The school cites its great success in small-scale projects in other major cities.[79]

The values the school establishes in its students through their educational model are as follows:

Habits of Heart, Mind, and Hands

Inclusion—the practice of interacting with others in work and play no matter who they are or where they come from

Collaboration—working with others to complete a task and to achieve shared goals

---

79 Boggs School website: boggsschool.org/place-based-education.

Creativity—the ability to make new things or think of new ideas

Empathy—the ability to understand and share the feelings of others

Health—the practice of making choices that promote ones mental, emotional, and physical well-being

Mastery—a level of great skill developed after continuous effort

Grit—the continuous effort of working through challenging tasks

Self determination—the practice of having a goal oriented and self-directing mindset

Resourcefulness—the ability to overcome problems or make do with what is available to create a solution

Critical thinking—disciplined thinking that is clear, rational, open-minded, and informed by evidence

In short, the school seeks to create participants in building Beloved Community in the city of Detroit.

A Different Model

As opposed to other chapters in this book, this chapter does not have sections on "the challenges they faced / how they overcame them." The reason is this:

- By the assessment of the Detroit Summer organizers, the challenge their community faced was the shadow side of capitalism, or what the organization Movement Generation refers to as "the extraction economy" which extracts what it can from both land and laborers;
- The process of overcoming such a massive system as the extraction economy is a decades-long task; and
- Their greatest challenge remains ahead of them: gentrification in Detroit.

Detroit is not the first city to face the challenge of low-income community members banding together to beautify their community, reduce crime, increase youth opportunities, and then become desirable enough that wealthier people want to move in, pushing prices up and displacing residents and businesses who can no longer afford to stay. In fact, the Dudley Street Neighborhood Initiative intentionally implemented strategies that would either not allow or would discourage gentrification in their community. Urban planners create culture-specific neighborhood improvements in a small attempt to decrease the likelihood of gentrification and displacement in culture-specific neighborhoods. (For example, one Chinese immigrant community made sure to put in a concrete park suitable to their community's popular tai chi classes, in contrast to the grass-and-tree park the city might otherwise have put in, which would have made the neighborhood more of a draw for non-Chinese people seeking affordable rent and proximity to public transit.)

Because Detroit's population has dropped from its height of 1.86 million people in 1950 to 700,000 today, some people see Detroit, which filed for bankruptcy in 2013, as a wasteland that people are doing a favor when they come and create new businesses. And yet, as one resident noted, "When people come to Detroit they see Detroit as a blank canvas and a blank slate, and it does become opportunistic, because people will say, "Oh, it's a playground!" People think it's a place where you can do whatever you want to. But that's not true. It's not a blank canvas, because that assumes that nobody lives here, and we still we have around 700,000 people living here."[80] In downtown Detroit, longtime Black-owned businesses are being closed down as high end white-owned businesses are garnering leases. The salt in the wound is that the media refers to this as "the New Detroit," which was a phrase a number of people connected to Detroit Summer had been using as much as a decade earlier to describe the self-sustaining community-based model of a new local economy they sought

---

80 Kristen Doerer, "What people not from Detroit need to know about Detroit," *PBS NewsHour,* July 1, 2016, pbs.org.

to create. It is not yet clear what the influx of new money into the city's downtown will mean for the longtime residents investing in creating a different version of Detroit grounded in radical self-sufficiency, deep commitment to community, and participation in the healing all those harmed by systems of injustice, including the work of healing the earth.

Solutions Employed

This chapter also did not include a "here's a specific tool they used in the healing of their neighborhood" section. There are three things that all the examples from this chapter have in common, though:

- Solutions stayed deeply connected to the earth.
- Solutions factored in both the needs and gifts of community members.
- Solutions stayed local, and they stayed reliant on community members to create and sustain them.

Sometimes people seeking to participate in justice move to a place receptive to their values or a place with enough space for them to innovate. That is part of what has caused the current tensions in Detroit: young entrepreneurs and innovators seeking a "blank canvas" without recognizing how they are painting over someone else's canvas. Sometimes people do not believe their own community has the skills to address the problems they face. This is why nonprofits receive funding to bring in outside experts to solve the problem of crime in a community and do not see crime significantly drop. The community that came together to create Detroit Summer and its successor programs had a different approach: trust relationship. Trust people's lived experiences as the cornerstone for creating solutions to the community's problems. And trust the earth to be able to bring people together as a starting place for the world of building a more resilient community…a Beloved Community.

As Grace Lee Boggs said, "the most radical thing I ever did was to stay put." She invited all people to do the same: stay local. Do the work with your neighbors, your people, whoever they are, rejecting the pioneer notion that can displace others but that also uproots existing communities that need hometown innovators. "We urgently need to bring to our communities the limitless capacity to love, serve, and create for and with each other. We urgently need to bring the neighbor back into our hoods, not only in our inner cities but also in our suburbs, our gated communities, on Main Street and Wall Street, and on Ivy League campuses," said Boggs in her book *The Next American Revolution*. We have work to do where we have been planted. That work can be amazing, wherever it is.

After all, "[t]here's something about people beginning to seek solutions by doing things for themselves," noted Grace Lee Boggs at the age of 96, "by deciding they are going to create new concepts of economy, new concepts of governance, new concepts of education, and that they have the capacity within themselves to do that, that we have that capacity to create the world anew. I mean, if you lived in Detroit or if you came to Detroit more often, you would be absolutely amazed at the people who start to create solutions to everyday problems and, in doing so, create movements."[81]

LEARN MORE

To learn about the technical aspects of creating community transformation (starting with a community garden), check out the toolkit "The New Barn Raising" by Gareth Potts based on research in Detroit, Minneapolis/St. Paul and Baltimore to effect policy change to address community and civic asset use for community well-being: gmfus.org/publications/new-barn-raising.

For a deep dive into the philosophy that can turn community gardening into an act of revolution, particularly in the midst of blight and despair in a largely abandoned community, read Grace Lee Boggs's *The Next American Revolution: Sustainable Activism for the Twenty-First Century*, May 2012, University of California Press.

For a starting place in connecting gardens to community renewal, Boggs's interview with Bill Moyers in 2007: pbs.org, or vimeo.com/33217407, or the rich interview by Krista Tippett in

---

81 *On Being* interview, Aug. 27, 2015, onbeing.org.

her radio show episode from On Being: onbeing.org/programs/
grace-lee-boggs-a-century-in-the-world.

To learn more on indigenous wisdom regarding plants, read
*Braiding Sweetgrass: Indigenous Wisdom, Scientific Knowledge,
and the Teachings of Plants,* Robin Wall Kimmerer, Milkweed
Editions, 2014.

To understand the damage that mass incarceration has done
to the fabric of Black America, Black American families, and to the
United States of America as a whole, read Michelle Alexander's
The New Jim Crow, the New Press, 2010 or watch the film *13ᵗʰ*,
2016, directed by Ava DuVarney, available through Netflix. For
some powerful solutions, look up the book *Locking Up Our Own:
Crime and Punishment in Black America,* James Forman, Jr., Farrar,
Straus and Giroux, 2017.

NOTE: This chapter used the term "Beloved Community"
several times without defining it. First coined by late nineteenth/
early twentieth century philosopher Josiah Royce, the term was
popularized by the Rev. Dr. Martin Luther King, Jr. According
to the King Center, "For Dr. King, The Beloved Community was
not a lofty utopian goal to be confused with the rapturous image
of the Peaceable Kingdom, in which lions and lambs coexist in
idyllic harmony. Rather, The Beloved Community was for him
a realistic, achievable goal that could be attained by a critical
mass of people committed to and trained in the philosophy and
methods of nonviolence.

Dr. King's Beloved Community is a global vision, in which
all people can share in the wealth of the earth. In the Beloved
Community, poverty, hunger and homelessness will not be
tolerated because international standards of human decency will
not allow it. Racism and all forms of discrimination, bigotry and
prejudice will be replaced by an all-inclusive spirit of sisterhood
and brotherhood. In the Beloved Community, international disputes
will be resolved by peaceful conflict-resolution and reconciliation
of adversaries, instead of military power. Love and trust will
triumph over fear and hatred. Peace with justice will prevail over
war and military conflict." This term and Dr. King's expanded
framework for it resonated deeply with Grace Lee Boggs and
continues to resonate deeply with many peacemakers and
community builders today.

9

The Power of Rooted Faith

We are a mirror of the gift of life in that we can make the
choice to give ourselves to a cause and to a way of life that is
much larger than we are. We can give ourselves to a work that
we will never succeed in fulfilling.

— REV. JAMES LAWSON, JR.

Peace is not the product of terror or fear.
Peace is not the silence of cemeteries.
Peace is not the silent result of violent repression.
Peace is the generous, tranquil contribution of all to the good
*   of all.*
Peace is dynamism.
Peace is generosity.
It is right and it is duty.

—**ARCHBISHOP OSCAR ROMERO**

I have worked hard to create in these pages a resource that will serve
people regardless of whether they have any particular faith convictions
or not, and regardless of what those faith convictions are. Much of
my work is done in secular settings and it is powerful work. That
said, I am the daughter of a Hindu father and Scottish Presbyterian
mother, and spirituality does shape both who I am and how I imagine
possibilities in the world. The organizing work I love doing most,
which helps me position myself for a long-term justice movement, is
shaped by my faith. So I wanted to share with you my own experiences
in transforming community which have happened through a model
of organizing called faith-rooted organizing. This chapter is written
through a primarily Christian lens; I hope you will find aspects of it
relevant to your own worldview. And I also invite you to explore the
book Faith-Rooted Organizing *by my friend and mentor Alexia*

Salvatierra and Peter Heltzel for more details, and to look for videos
online where Alexia talks about this model. She formalized this model
with the Rev. James Lawson, one of the powerful nonviolent organizers
of the civil rights movement in the U.S. in the 1960s, and it is
influenced by that movement as well as Gandhi's Satyagraha movement
in India and Latin American liberation theology of the 1970s and 80s.

We can't say for sure what caused the sheriff to change
his policy. We had been trying to meet with him for months.

Immigration rights organizations had reached out,
picketed, protested, collected petitions, testified at county
board meetings. They made sure he knew that in this very
diverse county, his participation with Immigration and
Customs Enforcement to detain nonviolent immigrants
overnight so they could deport them was unacceptable.
Tearing apart families as well as the local economy,
traumatizing children, was unacceptable. In fact, the day
before he had been visited by a fierce and dedicated group
of young activists led by the Dreamers, the undocumented
youth and young adults who have been staging acts of
resistance across the country even at risk of deportation, and
he made it clear he was irritated by them.

It could just be that he got worn down.

But the day he got worn down, well, it was a day that
felt like a little bit of a miracle, and by miracle, I mean it was
the day that something we had begun to believe might be
impossible proved possible.

Preparing to go into the sheriff's office yet again, one of
the religious leaders in the group, a Buddhist man who didn't
have the papers that would allow him to stay in this country,
suggested the group pause in silent meditation and prayer
before what would likely be another fruitless visit. Dozens
of people of faith sat in the grass beneath the sheriff's office
window and prayed silently for God's presence to open the
heart of the sheriff. The group prayed fervently because
prayer was about all that was left.

And that particular day, the sheriff finally met with the
religious contingent to receive our letter in person and to

hear our words of witness. And that week, he expressed an openness to supporting the TRUST Act, an act that would decrease costly immigration "holds" for nonviolent undocumented immigrants so that ICE could get to them in time to deport them.[82]

***

We can't say that God intervened. We can't even say the sheriff was shamed into it by witnessing people silently praying. What we know is we spent months trying to make him see reason, and one day the Catholic sheriff finally agreed to hear the testimonies of faith leaders who are watching our current immigration policies tear apart families and perpetuate economic violence in our communities.

Disruptive Action

I remember the first time I participated in an action with Faith Alliance for a Moral Economy (FAME), about seven or eight years ago. I had mentioned that I care a lot about workers' rights, and FAME organizer Kristi Laughlin said, "we have an action happening this weekend—it brings together environmentalists, workers and low-income community members dealing with pollution in their neighborhood. It's kind of throwing you in at the deep end, because this campaign has been going on a long time and doesn't look likely to end any time soon, so this is a really disruptive action. If you don't want to go, I understand."

I wasn't going to admit I was scared, so I showed up in front of Oakland city hall wearing my stole.[83] And while I had been involved in social justice work (even faith-based social justice work) for years, I could tell this was something different. Environmentalists and union workers

---

82 The purpose of this chapter isn't to wade too deeply into policy issues. If you are interested in reading more about the Trust Act, there is a fairly detailed article in *Huffington Post* called "Trust Act Signed In California To Limit Deportation Program" that gets at the technical issues. For an elegant theological reflection on immigration, visit https://www.americamagazine.org/issue/763/article/theology-migration for the article "A Theology of Migration: A new method for understanding a God on the move," by Daniel Groody.

83 A stole is the piece of fabric that Christian clergy wear, sometimes over a robe, sometimes not, that resembles a long scarf. It symbolizes the yoke, like a cow's yoke, to remind clergy that they are servants of the people they encounter.

(Black and South Asian Sikh and Latino arm in arm) and community members of low-income mostly Black west Oakland marched in with rabbis and pastors to take over a port commission meeting to demand dignity for the drivers who had been forced into being independent contractors. Independent contractor status means the company no longer has responsibility for owning or maintaining trucks, passing on both maintenance and environmental improvement costs to the drivers while also not having to cover insurance or provide basic quality of life conditions for the drivers.

The mix of people in that action wasn't the only thing that helped me realize FAME was doing something different, although I had never seen that particular intersection of people in one movement before. Something else struck me even more powerfully. The pastor who took the mic at the commission meeting let them know that the commissioners had repeatedly refused to sit down and hear the stories of the workers, so the workers had come to the commission. He let them tell their stories in Punjabi and Spanish and English. He let members of the community speak their grief about children in the neighborhood breathing in toxic fumes and living with asthma because the trucks had to idle in their neighborhood for hours or else they might lose the contracting job that would put food on their tables. And then he said to the commissioners whose meeting we had disrupted, "we love you, though. We are here in love. We are here because we believe in your basic goodness and so we knew you needed to hear these stories in order to do God's will." And as we marched out chanting "Good jobs, clean air!" the chant I heard was "we love you, though."

***

My friend Kristi uses two quotes back-to-back to illustrate the difference between community organizing that happens in faith communities because of their people power on the one hand and faith-rooted organizing on the other, which is grounded in the compassionate depths of our faith traditions:

- "The thirteenth rule: Pick the target, freeze it, personalize it and polarize it." (Alinsky)

- "Nonviolent resistance is not for cowards. It is not a quiet, passive acceptance of evil. One is passive and nonviolent physically, but very active spiritually, always seeking ways to persuade the opponent of advantages to the way of love, cooperation, and peace....The goal is not to defeat or humiliate the opponent but rather to win him or her over to understanding new ways to create cooperation and community." (Gandhi)

***

Saul Alinsky is sometimes nicknamed the father of U.S.-based community organizing (although I imagine a number of civil rights leaders and suffragists and abolitionists would beg to differ). He recognized the power of organizing in faith communities because of all the people who, if mobilized, could force change. He recognized how ugly and brutal power was when wielded by people not held accountable for their actions, and he met power with power.

Gandhi obviously understood power differently. One might call it the power of persuasion, but in many ways it was more about a commitment to recognizing the divine in the other person.

For much of my life, I was far more focused on outcomes than on process, so this distinction would not have interested me as much as the policy wins involved with one approach versus another.

But at this point I find myself realizing that over the past several decades, we have been putting in more and more effort to achieve smaller and smaller wins. The "meet power with power" model isn't working because social and political structures are in place that ensure poor people and people of color will always have less power.

As a result, I've begun recognizing that process is a much more important part of the social justice movement than I fully realized. And the way in which we engage each other is part of how we redefine power.

Connecting Our Power

And this is where the subject of salvation comes in, I think. "Salvation" is a term frequently used within my Christian faith as if we all mean the same thing by it. I'm not sure we do, though.

I am part of a small Protestant denomination, the Disciples of Christ. Our claim to fame is that we were the first denomination founded on U.S. soil, and ours is a weirdly American tradition. There were Black and white Disciples from the very founding of our tradition, but in some of those churches the Black people were slaves in attendance with their white masters and often had to sit in the balcony. When prominent Black businessman and Disciples pastor Preston Taylor helped to establish a separately run and organized movement for Black Disciples in order to ensure that Black Disciples would no longer be treated as second class members of the Disciples of Christ, he said the following at their inaugural convention in 1917:

"The Disciples of Christ, strange as it may seem, need the colored people, if for no other reason, as the acid test of Christian orthodoxy and willingness to follow the Christ all of the way in His program of human redemption. For if the white brother can include in his religious theory and practice the colored people as real brothers he will have avoided the heresy of all heresies."

Our salvation is wrapped up in one another. The increasingly popular phrase from southern Africa is "Ubuntu," which is roughly translated to "I am because you are," or "I am because we are." It is used by people of all faiths in southern Africa because it is so spiritually resonant across faith traditions. I imagine Preston Taylor received some pushback for seeming to remove Black Disciples from an integrated movement. I imagine that quote above as his response, another way of saying this: our interconnectedness is not enough to connect us to God. It is our interconnectedness *where we honor each other as equally valued and equally to be supported* that connects us to God. Unequal relationships *are not of God.*

In that moment in history, White Disciples were not capable of partnering to create governing systems and structures and operations that upheld the dignity and worth of all of God's children equally. Preston Taylor's gift to Black Disciples was also his gift to White Disciples: the opportunity to work towards that equality so that they would not do interconnectedness in oppressive ways.

Whenever I talk about the principle of Ubuntu in public settings, people seem to feel really heart-warmed and inspired by the end of my talks.

I think I might be talking about it wrong.

And I think I've figured out why.

Visually, we picture racial reconciliation as breaking down a wall, but really it's moving a tall building with no staircases or elevators from vertical to horizontal so that people who could not move from floor to floor can now climb out the windows and meet each other for real. (And in that image, people get bumped around as the building tilts the full 90 degrees, and the folks on the top floor take a pretty big tumble.)[84]

In a church, mosque, gurdwara, synagogue or temple where people seek comfort rather than challenge, the good news of Ubuntu isn't particularly good news, because it is such hard work. But this is what compels me about both the faith community praying for the sheriff and Preston Taylor's statement from 100 years ago: they illustrate the theological power of doing the hard work.

One of my mentors is the Rev. Phil Lawson, a civil rights leader who was particularly active with Fellowship of Reconciliation and continues to advocate for the spiritual discipline of nonviolence as part of the justice movement. He once said to me, "A characteristic of empire is its ability to co-opt everybody. The Beloved Community is not about good feelings. It is not about whether 'you like me.' It is about demographics. It's about evaluating who's at the bottom of the ladder, and who is not at the table. Slavery was never an issue of, 'Do you like me?' It was an issue of a system that some people are worth more than others. And that has not changed."[85]

Within progressive Christian circles, much of our talk is about dismantling systems, which is critical if you agree

---

84 This image of the building tilting and the resulting anger of the people on the top floors makes me think of a saying growing in popularity these days: "when all you've known is advantage, equality feels a lot like oppression."

85 Sandhya Jha, *Pre-Post-Racial America* (St. Louis: Chalice Press, 2015), 19.

with Rev. Lawson that the systems in which we function are structured so that some people are worth more than others.

Our *talk* is about dismantling systems. Our *actions* tend to be about getting some people access to a little bit more within those systems. And I don't really apologize for that. One of the victories I am proudest of from my whole organizing career was at the former Oakland Army Base. A coalition of community organizations, youth organizations, environmental organizations, faith organizations and unions came together to advocate for this: when the former Oakland Army Base was repurposed for shipping by the Port of Oakland, the city should make sure that:

- half of the construction jobs and also half of the permanent jobs would go to Oakland residents,
- that barriers to entry (such as a history of incarceration) would be eliminated,
- that the work not further harm the already heavily polluted west Oakland neighborhood, and
- that people with barriers to employment would be trained in union-track jobs so that they could actually earn a living wage and be able to afford to stay in their community and raise their family here instead of being displaced as so many other low-income residents had been.

In a city where some neighborhoods see unemployment rates near 40 percent partly because formerly incarcerated people who have "paid their debt to society" continue to pay that debt by not being able to get jobs or housing, that was a really big win. Considering we were going up against the biggest developer in the world and that our city officials were terrified to alienate any business interests when the economy of our city was so fragile, and considering no one had *ever* guaranteed that kind of jobs agreement in the country up to that point (an agreement that included permanent jobs and not just construction jobs for local residents), it was a spectacular win.

But that win didn't change the system; it just helped a few thousand people get a little bit more within the system that they wouldn't have gotten otherwise.

In other words, it's not our salvation. It saves a few people, but it doesn't save a people. It liberates a few people from economic hardship, but it doesn't liberate a whole people from the economic system that put many of them in prison in the first place or that means many of them have access to far inferior educational opportunities than others.

***

I think it is critical to name that faith-rooted organizing does not presume that the faith community should be the only group doing organizing, or that we should ever do it alone. It is grounded in the principle of "multi-sectoral organizing" practiced so powerfully in the Philippines, where a robust justice movement has everyone organizing from their great strengths. Students, mothers, field workers, factory workers, faith communities all organize together with each group doing what they do best. This is a huge relief to me: I don't have to be a policy expert, a legal expert, and a labor organizer as well as bringing the spiritual gifts of my community. I can let the policy wonks, the lawyers and the labor organizers do those parts. In fact, that was part of the power of the moment with the with the sheriff at the beginning of this chapter: students and domestic workers and immigration attorneys had already been organizing alongside us in the days leading up to our visit to his office. It worked because we worked together, each bringing our best gifts.

***

So here's why I see faith-rooted organizing wrapped up in the issue of salvation. Here's how I saw salvation show up in that campaign:

- At a critical point in the campaign for good jobs at the army base, it looked like the coalition might unravel. The unions could negotiate with the developer and get everything they wanted without the rest of the coalition. Some community organizations worried that others in the coalition were too quick to negotiate or trust people with power. People worried that one organization or another was getting too much credit or too much attention or promoting themselves as the "lead" organization. A clergy colleague of mine, at a really tense meeting of the key stakeholders, said, "Wait. I'm going to ask us to pause for a minute. I'm going to ask us to picture the people who we're advocating for. I'm going to ask of us to think of them by name, by face. Let's remember who brought us into the room. Let's remember who brought us together to work side by side for all of the issues: union jobs, jobs for people returning from prison, opportunities for our young people who have no future in this city otherwise, and environmental justice for our city." The long, prayerful pause re-grounded the leaders and in a way, saved the coalition.

- My colleague Kristi and I organized a prayer vigil before an important city council meeting. We wove into it testimonies from people facing hopelessness due to lack of job opportunities. We lifted up prayers for our city and its people, passionate and heartfelt prayers from different cultures and faiths. We prayed over the people going in to testify, praying that spiritual power would resonate through them as they spoke, even if they never once mentioned faith in their testimony. We broke bread and shared it, acknowledging that all of our traditions spoke to the sharing of resources. Afterwards, the speakers said even though they had testified about this campaign several times, the energy this time was different. They were grounded in their power. They were grounded in hope. They were able to be calm and passionate all at once. They carried our prayers into city council.

- When things were getting desperate, a couple of the community organizations staged an impromptu sit-in at the global headquarters of the developer who refused to meet with community leaders and would only work with the city (and only if we were not at the table). We asked to meet with the director, and we sat in the lobby as we waited. It was awkward and uncomfortable because the people keeping us from the director were people who would probably have benefitted from the kind of proposal we were bringing. When things escalated, one of the community organizers asked me to pray, and I did. While we waited fruitlessly, one of the youth said he had been watching "Eyes on the prize" and asked us to sing "Ain't Gonna Let Nobody Turn Us Around" ("gonna keep on walking, keep on talking, marching to that freedom land"). It made us a little less scared as we waited for security or police, even though it echoed through that huge foyer and drew crowds of employees to see what the fuss was about. We didn't get arrested (for which I was grateful: a young family had come to serve as witness to who these jobs would help, and I didn't know what would have happened to the beautiful toddler). We didn't get to meet with the director, although his assistant heard our testimony and took our letter of petition. But soon after that the city arranged for strategizing meetings between city staff, the developer *and coalition leaders*, which moved the stalled process forward again.[86]

- During the campaign, people were grateful to see the faith community showing up for something that affected them directly instead of only once they were dead. Too often they had seen the religious community care more about their personal morals than about the violence and injustice that harmed them every day. (To quote Oakland-based hip hop group, The Coup, "Preacherman wanna save my soul; don't nobody wanna save my life. People we done lost control. Let's make heaven tonight.") And people felt emboldened to claim their own faith to strengthen them as they

---

86 As a side note, this action was another illustration of multi-sectoral organizing. These types of tactics did not sit well with some of the more cautious organizations in the coalition. The agreement reached was that one organization did this action in their own name and not on behalf of the whole coalition; agitation was the gift of this group. And they made sure to have faith leaders with them to bring gifts of prayer and music. Maybe this helped the massive international corporation come back to the bargaining table with the coalition, if only to avoid more prayer and singing and young parents with their toddlers in the main office.

took big leaps in speaking out against injustice. It was a little glimpse into what made the civil rights movement powerful: people were allowed to rely on their faith to bolster them, even if it meant they were being bolder sometimes than their own faith leaders and definitely bolder than the faith community as a whole.

A completely secular campaign might have won the same victories (although it might have unraveled without a voice calling it back into unity and solidarity). A faith-based campaign might have incorporated songs and prayers for dramatic effect. But because of the influence of faith-rooted organizing, people in the movement relocated their understanding of where power lies. It lies in our courage. It lies in being supported by something much bigger than us that stretches across all of history. And a faith-rooted campaign helped people recognize their spiritual power to confront traditional power and also to build something completely different.

Defending Truth and the Weak

There's one more thing about faith-rooted organizing that I see as critical to our work of collective salvation. It's how the faith community is kept honest in the process. Because as Rev. Phil reminds us, "Beloved Community" is about justice and access and voice, not just about whether I like you.

Workers at a country club in the San Francisco suburbs were locked out of their jobs a few years ago for not agreeing to a truly unjust contract with management. What this meant in practice was that those who stood with their union showed up for work one day to discover they were not allowed to work or collect any wages even though they had done nothing other than try to negotiate the exact same contract they had negotiated in previous years.[87]

In addition to being financially devastating for workers who relied on a fair wage job to support families, their

---

87 Another campaign aside: one of the people they locked out was a janitor who had found a memo in the new manager's trash can noting that one of his goals was to eliminate the union, who had not engaged in a labor dispute in the decades they had been in place at the country club.

campaign to get their jobs back taught them some painful realities about the people for whom they worked. The workers were vilified and derided by some country club members; even members who supported them wouldn't do so publicly because the one member who did was blackballed and shunned. During one picket, a member biked by with a baby stroller attached to her bike. The toddler stuck his hand out of the stroller to give the workers a thumbs down. The mother had trained her child to taunt the workers.

Leading up to Mother's Day, they engaged in a three-day fast for worker justice to remind people that working mothers were being hurt by the unjust contract which suddenly made them pay their own health care (which constituted up to 40 percent of their pay if they had children, during a record breaking earnings year for the club). While they stood in front of the clubhouse handing out flyers on the third day of their fast, one country club member spat at a worker that the worker was tearing apart families because the member's son wouldn't cross their picket line to have Mother's Day brunch. The worker this member spat at had adopted three children the day before she was locked out of her job. Talk about tearing apart families.

On Good Friday, clergy gathered across the road from the golf course to do a foot-washing of the workers' feet, acknowledging their dignity. Most of the clergy wouldn't speak out in favor of the workers, because they had country club members in their pews and didn't want to alienate them. The workers were aware of this and hurt by it. And as the clergy read scriptures that honored the dignity of "the least of these," a worker came to the megaphone. He had been on the picket line for a year, locked out of a job he wanted to do as long as he was compensated fairly for his work. His church hadn't shown up for him because the priest did not want to get involved in politics. His salary had supported his sister's family struggling at home in Mexico, and the whole extended family was suffering. Through translation, he read Jeremiah 22:13–17:

"Woe to him who builds his palace by unrighteousness,
    his upper rooms by injustice,
making his own people work for nothing,
    not paying them for their labor.
He says, 'I will build myself a great palace
    with spacious upper rooms.'
So he makes large windows in it,
    panels it with cedar
    and decorates it in red.

"Does it make you a king
    to have more and more cedar?
Did not your father have food and drink?
    He did what was right and just,
    so all went well with him.
He defended the cause of the poor and needy,
    and so all went well.
Is that not what it means to know me?"
    declares the Lord.
"But your eyes and your heart
    are set only on dishonest gain,
on shedding innocent blood
    and on oppression and extortion."

And in reading that passage, he shamed those pastors who would not speak out publicly, who would not sign letters in the local paper or show up to city council meetings even when the city's mayor publicly supported the workers. He didn't do it harshly. He didn't even use his own words. He just reminded them that God stood stronger for the dignity of workers than they did. That day, he was the most powerful faith leader in the group, and he taught all of us about what it meant to be people of faith in a Good Friday world.

For me, that's at the heart of the salvific power of faith-rooted organizing. As under-sung hero of the civil rights movement Ella Baker famously said, "Strong people don't need strong leaders." Faith-rooted organizing reminded our elected officials of who their best selves are. And long before we ever get in front of those officials, it is about us reminding each other and ourselves of who our best selves are. Faith-rooted organizing is about the saving of our communities in the here and now by nurturing us into collaborative leadership to build up an alternative community with an alternative way of navigating power. It is about ultimately creating new systems where everyone's gifts are honored and everyone's needs are met, and where there are no enemies or "targets."

***

I do not want to romanticize faith-rooted organizing as if it has magical results. The sheriff I mentioned has reverted to participating with immigration and customs officials. People of faith recently hosted a footwashing in front of his office hoping to tap into his faith convictions. They are also continuing to mobilize community resistance in this area that takes pride in its commitment to supporting immigrants who do not pose any threat to our safety and who contribute to the social fabric of our county. It has been a real roller coaster because the sheriff is celebrated by important people in Washington, D.C., for defying his community's desires, and he still does not consistently feel in his heart the spiritual dissonance of his actions.

***

In these moments, I take comfort from a story I have heard Alexia tell many times during the faith-rooted organizing trainings she facilitates.

When she was a community organizer in the Philippines, she worked with some amazing women who were demanding the factory they worked at compensate them fairly and give them safe working conditions. As a small act of resistance, the women planted banana trees by their housing compound so they could better feed their children.

When they came back from work, the company had razed the banana trees with bulldozers. The women wept. And then they got back to organizing.

Alexia asked how they could keep going when every effort got torn down.

"Because we'll win soon," they responded.

"How can you say that? This will take years!" Alexia protested.

"Yes. Soon," they agreed. "Our daughters' daughters will see victory. Soon."

***

Faith-rooted organizing is a practice that works across many faith traditions. At its core, it is about these things:

- Appealing to the common good (transcending "self-interest")
- The distinct contributions of faith communities to multi-sectoral organizing (working alongside other powerful organizing bodies and bringing the best of our faith traditions to the broader movement, as recently made famous by the Rev. Dr. William Barber of North Carolina):
  - Moral imagination and inspiration
  - Chaplaincy (care of people on the front lines)
  - Circle of care (faith communities prepared to act in support of workers, immigrants, others being targeted)
  - Shared language of hope (words from our many sacred texts that ground people in the possibilities of committing ourselves to justice)
  - Symbolic resources (like the prayer vigil before the city council meeting)

When we bring the best of our traditions, the unifying and transcendent aspects of our faith, it can offer strength and encouragement and hope to others working with us on building a world where all people can thrive.

The Lord's Prayer is written in the first-person plural. We're trained to hear it and pray it in the first person singular, as if it's just about me, as if it says, "My father who art in heaven" instead of "Our father." And I think that matters to the issue of salvation. It matters to what kind of community we're building up. It matters to Preston Taylor's point about how people of color would save White people because honoring the full humanity and siblinghood of people of color was at the heart of White people's salvation (or as he worded it, "avoiding the greatest of heresies").

And the next line, the one we breeze by without thinking too much about it, is also critical to why I think faith-rooted organizing is essential to our collective salvation, and why I define salvation a little differently than the preacherman the Coup talks about: "Thy kingdom come, thy will be done *on earth as it is in heaven.*" Jesus invites us to build up the realm of God here and now. In my Christian tradition, Jesus invites us to make heaven tonight.

Or, as my favorite Hindu poet, Rabindranath Tagore, puts it equally eloquently:

Leave this chanting and singing and telling of beads!
Whom dost thou worship in this lonely dark corner
  of a temple with doors all shut?
Open thine eyes and see thy God is not before thee!

He is there where the tiller is tilling the hard ground
  and where the pathmaker is breaking stones.
He is with them in sun and in shower,
  and his garment is covered with dust.
Put off thy holy mantle and even like him
  come down on the dusty soil!

Deliverance? Where is this deliverance to be found?
Our master himself has joyfully taken upon him
  the bonds of creation;
he is bound with us all for ever.

Come out of thy meditations
  and leave aside thy flowers and incense!
What harm is there if thy clothes become tattered and
  stained?
Meet him and stand by him in toil and in sweat of thy
  brow.

May we find our salvation through one another. May we be faith-rooted and not just faith-based. And may we together make heaven tonight.

10

The Power of Being Who We've Been Taught to Be

"The duty of Christians is to resist the violence that will be brought to bear on their consciences through the weapons of the spirit. We will resist whenever our adversaries will demand of us obedience contrary to the orders of the gospel. We will do so without fear but also without pride and without hate."

—PROCLAMATION BY PASTOR ANDRÉ TROCMÉ IN WORSHIP, JUNE 3, 1940, THE DAY AFTER FRANCE SIGNED AN ARMISTICE WITH NAZI GERMANY

"Nobody asked who was Jewish and who was not. Nobody asked where you were from. Nobody asked who your father was or if you could pay. They just accepted each of us, taking us in with warmth, sheltering children, often without their parents—children who cried in the night from nightmares."

—ELIZABETH KOENIG-KAUFMAN, A FORMER CHILD REFUGEE IN LE CHAMBON

In my first year of seminary, we studied theological ethics and how it applied to public life. I think we were studying a famous 14th-century ethicist whose teachings seemed pretty abstract to me. "That's fine in theory," I said to one of my professors, "but how does that get translated to the people in church in ways that actually make a difference…not just to how they treat the grocery store clerk, but to the way they build a community?"

My professor barely looked up from his notes. "Read *Lest Innocent Blood Be Shed* and then we can talk."

It's been about 15 years since I read that book and what I remembered about the story was this: the pastor of the

French village of Le Chambon consistently preached *prior to* and throughout World War II that to be Christian means protecting the innocent. That meant that by the time the Nazi-supporting Vichy government had taken over France, the congregation was conditioned to do what was right even at cost to themselves.

As I revisited the book, along with a famous documentary by the son of a Jewish survivor from Le Chambon and several articles, I realized the story was richer but not much more complicated than that.

There's one scene in the book that captures the essence of that community's "organizing strategy" to me. It occurs after pastor André Trocmé and his flock have been housing Jewish refugees for several years and the village's chief of police and his officers show up at the pastor's door one evening, clearly with the intent of taking Pastor Trocmé to a prison camp. The pastor's wife, Magda, invites them in and also invites the officers to join them for dinner.

Later, friends would say to her, "How could you bring yourself to sit down to eat with these men who were there to take your husband away, perhaps to his death? How could you be so forgiving, so decent to them?"

> To such questions she always gave the same answer: "What are you talking about? It was dinnertime; they were standing in my way; we were all hungry. The food was ready. What do you mean by such foolish words as 'forgiving' and 'decent'?"[88]

The interesting thing about André Trocmé is that his goal was not to rescue Jewish people. His goal was to build a community founded on the principles of nonviolence. He had grown up witnessing the horrible ramifications of World War I when his own village was occupied by the Germans and had learned young that there are victims on all sides in war. His heart had been changed in particular by his interactions with German soldiers led through his town growing up; he knew them as the enemy but also witnessed them missing body parts, faces torn up beyond recognition from the shrapnel

---

88 Philip P. Hallie, *Lest Innocent Blood Be Shed* (New York: Harper, 1994), 20.

of WWI. In particular, his sense of enemies was derailed in the following exchange: a German soldier staying in his home (occupied as military quarters) extended a kindness to him, which he rejected, saying "You are an enemy…. You wear that uniform, and tomorrow you will perhaps kill my brother, who is a French soldier fighting against you, trying to get you Germans out of our country. Why have you come into our country carrying war and suffering and misery?"

"I am not what you think," the soldier answered. "I am a Christian…at Breslau we found Christ, and we have given him our life….I shall not kill your brother; I shall kill no Frenchman. God has revealed to us that a Christian must not kill, ever. We never carry arms."[89]

He went on to explain that as a telegrapher, he was supposed to carry a pistol but just took the risk of being shot.

When Trocmé arrived as pastor in Le Chambon 20 years later, he was struck by the fact that outside of tourist season, there was no industry to provide life and vitality to the community. He eventually landed on the vision of a school that might actually move the struggling villagers' children toward college, and where he would be free to teach his vision of nonviolence in a way he could not have through the existing public school in the village.

The school grew quickly after its launch in 1938, partly because of the refugees arriving from central and eastern Europe (Spanish people and Nazi opposition folks as well as Jewish people from Germany and Austria), some of whom became students and some of whom were utilized as needed teachers in that rural outpost.

And each Sunday, Trocmé and his associate preached a message of nonviolence and of caring for those in need to his flock of Huguenot descendants.[90]

---

89 Hallie, *Lest Innocent*, 58.
90 According to the National Huguenot Society, "The Huguenots were French Protestants most of whom eventually came to follow the teachings of John Calvin, and who, due to religious persecution, were forced to flee France to other countries in the 16th and 17th centuries. Some remained, practicing their Faith in secret." This is important to the story of Le Chambon because a village of people grounded in their narrative of fleeing oppression were then placed in a position of helping those fleeing oppression. It also fostered a distrust of authoritarian regimes by the village and surrounding rural areas.

[T]heir sermons had another aspect: in attacking evil, we must cherish the preciousness of all human life. Our obligation to diminish the evil in the world must begin at home; we must not do evil, must not ourselves do harm. To be against evil is to be against the destruction of human life and against the passions that motivate that destruction.

But the sermons did not propose a neat blueprint for fighting hatred with love. They were not attempts to tell the world or Le Chambon exactly how to overcome Hitler's evil with love. In those last years of the 1930s, the sermons said: Work and look hard for ways, for opportunities to make little moves against destructiveness. The sermons did not tell what those moves should be; they said only that an imitator of Christ must somehow make such moves when the occasion arises. They were preaching an attitude of resistance and of canny, unsentimental watching for opportunities to do something tin the spirit of that resistance. Those opportunities soon came.[91]

***

In his film "Weapons of the Spirit," Pierre Sauvage returned to the village of Le Chambon where he was born to his Jewish Polish mother who had successfully fled and been sheltered there when most of her family was killed by Nazis. "The Nazis had proclaimed a thousand year Reich and appeared triumphant. *But for the people of Le Chambon, that was beside the point*," noted Sauvage. [italics mine]

When he interviewed some of the villagers, this fascinating conversation emerged: "We never asked for explanations. Nobody asked anything. When people came, if we could be of help...," said Henri Héritier, clearly uncomfortable with the attention of being filmed.

"But you were taking risks," Sauvage followed up, "in sheltering Jews."

"At first not so much," Héritier responded. "But towards the end it did start...becoming dangerous."

---

91 Hallie, *Lest Innocent*, 85.

"But you kept them anyhow?"

"Oh yes," said Héritier and his wife Emma.

"Why?"

"I don't know," said Mrs. Héritier, smiling a little. "We were used to it." And she shrugged slightly, still smiling.[92]

While their efforts were an open secret largely ignored by the Vichy regime, they did suffer losses because of their commitment:

> On June 29, 1943, the German police raided a local secondary school and arrested 18 students. The Germans identified five of them as Jews, and sent them to Auschwitz, where they died. The German police also arrested their teacher, Daniel Trocmé, Pastor Trocmé's cousin, and deported him to the Lublin/Majdanek concentration camp, where the SS killed him. Roger Le Forestier, Le Chambon's physician, who was especially active in helping Jews obtain false documents, was arrested and subsequently shot on August 20, 1944, in Montluc prison on orders of the Gestapo in Lyon.[93]

According to the Holocaust Encyclopedia, the village of 5,000 people plus another 24,000 people scattered across the surrounding plateau provided refuge for approximately 5,000 people fleeing the Vichy government and the Germans. This included somewhere between 3,000 and 3,500 Jewish people. They housed them, forged identification and ration cards, and guided some to neutral Switzerland, the same path their Huguenot ancestors had followed. (This earned them the nickname "that nest of Jews in Protestant country" by the Vichy police.)

While the other chapters in this book have focused on modern day efforts to create healthy, thriving communities, I wanted to begin and end with chapters that connected us to a history not-so-long past (although I could have chosen many examples much older), to remind us of something important:

---

92 My interpretation of a scene from the documentary *Weapons of the Spirit: Conspiracy of Goodness at Le Chambon-sur-Lignon* by Pierre Sauvage, 1987.

93 Holocaust Encyclopedia entry on Le Chambon-sur-Lignon: https://www.ushmm.org/wlc/en/article.php?ModuleId=10007518

for millennia, the world has thrown awful things at people and people have chosen to live into their core identities, in community, knowing there might be consequences but knowing they needed to do it anyhow.

Father Arizmendiarrietta was helping pick up the pieces in a beleaguered town in the Basque region of Spain in the wake of the Spanish Civil War which had been borne particularly hard by that region. The fascist regime of Spain loathed the independent-minded and democratically run Basque country, and they had done everything possible to crush the spirit of that community. Father Arizmendi had been imprisoned for the treason of writing in his own Basque language when serving as a war correspondent. Described as "an idealist with a practical bent," Father Arizmendi recognized that one thing could lift his community out of financial oppression and he helped get it set up through small group meetings to bring people on board. (He was an uncompelling public speaker whose church tried to get the bishop to move him, but he was great in small groups, and he leaned into his gifts.) The community of Mondragón was able to build up a cooperative system to support the whole village because they had baked into them the Basque culture of independence even at great cost, so they were willing to build up their own economy under the nose of Franco.

Pastor Trocmé also came to a village that upon his arrival he described as moving toward "death, death, death, and the pastor was entrusted with helping the village die."[94] He got a school going to create a college track for the children and also create educational opportunities for the adults during the non-tourist season. And he taught nonviolent principles at school and church, making sure the village understood that nonviolence was active in its efforts to create healing among people who are suffering. So when France began to cooperate with Nazi Germany, the village of Le Chambon knew how to live into their identities as refugees arrived in their village, even knowing it would potentially come at a cost. (They also remained true to their nonviolent commitments until almost the end of the war and some of

94 Hallie, *Lest Innocent*, 78.

them all the way through, because they also understood who they were called to be.)

Throughout this book are many stories in which, if you sat down with the people doing the work, the first thing they would say is, "you need to know, this is hard." In fact, when CamishaFatimah read the first draft of my chapter on restorative justice, she made me include things from our conversation that I had initially left out of the chapter: sometimes people don't want to do the work, and sometimes people think they want to do the work until they start doing it, and it turns out restorative justice models ask more than most people are willing to give. All of the stories in this book result in a messy version of community with some rough edges and a constant need to reevaluate and adjust in order to get at their overarching goals.[95]

And it is worlds better than the suffering and enmity and fear that these efforts have replaced.

What is also true of all of these stories is this: people creating change in their communities over time got really clear about who they were and who they understood their community to be, and that functioned as their lodestar throughout hard times. The people in the Dudley Street neighborhood remembered that their community was made up of people who deserved what other people got: parks that children can play in, no illegal dumping, spaces for intergenerational connections, and a path to affordable home ownership and business success...and not losing that community to wealthier folks once they had improved it.

Each of these stories also exhibits how process shaped outcome. There are a lot of political actions emerging these days, some of which are moving and energizing and contribute to people's sense that they are not alone when they feel isolated and scared. Some of these actions are *moments* that people can hold onto and treasure but which don't build towards anything concrete. Other actions are connected to *movements*. They involve strategy, and the

---

95 In fact, the Mondragon Corporation in the past few years has wrestled with wanting to remain competitive by outsourcing some work to Asia but not offering Asian workers worker-owner status. New challenges are always emerging to the core values of building Beloved Community.

public action is neither the beginning nor the end. A "Hands Around the Mosque" event after an attack on a mosque is a powerful *moment*. Intentional relationship building between members of the mosque and others in the community, maybe leading to creating a safety strategy in which others commit to protecting the mosque, and/or members of the mosque working with allies to create a commitment by the city officials to establish a safe city policy for religious inclusion, and/or creating a restorative justice program so that if people are caught defacing the mosque, they might have to learn the impact of that action and make more meaningful restitution than time in jail, that is a *movement* that builds over time. It is sustainable, it is not instantaneous, and it involves processes that cultivate trust and the ability to work together toward shared solutions that involve a broad array of voices while prioritizing the voices of those most affected by the harm happening in the community.

And building a movement requires *relationship*. The final component of each story is a willingness by the people who helped effect change is this: they had the courage to make their voice heard by decision makers and to work with them (Dudley Street), or they recognized their need to listen to people they had been trained to ignore (asset-based community development), or they kept showing up in spaces people had given up on, over and over, until community became inevitable (Recovery Café). They remained invested in each other. They remained invested in their place. They remained invested in their communities' possibilities in the face of real challenges, in the face of others having given up on them. And most importantly, *they didn't let ego get in the way of impact*. They made sure that their efforts were group efforts, bringing in multiple people's gifts and voices. The era of the great individual savior is over (if it ever really existed). Community matters more than charisma in building a sustainable movement. Even if that charisma is paired with a great vision, it is not enough to carry change across more than one generation. Community buy-in and community input make community work richer and longer standing.

As I mentioned at the beginning of this book, I am increasingly convinced we are at the beginning of a 50-year movement. As I see it from my years of organizing, what worked for labor rights and civil rights in the 20th century will not carry us forward today. We will need the wisdom of our ancestors more than our immediate predecessors. We will need to be about building community from the ground up, to re-ground our neighbors in the value of other-care that has been stripped away from us little by little, almost invisibly. (And to be clear, some of our immediate predecessors, especially unsung women like Fannie Lou Hamer, practiced these values long before this moment, but their wisdom was not institutionalized as it should have been.) We will need to help people around us address real threats (like skyrocketing violence towards people perceived as Muslim) more than perceived threats (like the unreasonable and statistically inaccurate fear of Muslims). We will need to understand our thriving as inextricable from each other's. It only took 50 years of intentional strategizing, starting small and building big, to create our current context. If we start now, what might we be able to create over the next 50 years? A country where children grow up to find and share their gifts instead of being consumed by the school-to-prison pipeline. A country where there is fresh food for everyone and people are in touch with the land and the water. A country where race and gender are not erased but do not dictate people's possibilities. If we start now, there is no end to what we might be in 50 years.

Even before this election I had a sense that building community needed to be the cornerstone of creating a nation invested in all of its people. At its best, all movement work is both connected to real people's lives and simultaneously oriented towards creating systems of justice that do not rely solely on whether you know and like me (to paraphrase Rev. Phil Lawson).

This book does not occur in a vacuum for me. Twelve years ago, I helped a congregation of 15 people figure out what they wanted to contribute to the city that had caused them so much pain but which they had chosen not to abandon (those who had a choice). We all knew what it meant to lose people to violence, to feel afraid in our own neighborhoods, to know a constant sense of instability. So it is not surprising that they chose to focus on creating peace. That is what led to, seven years later, the launch of the Oakland Peace Center. That small but faithful band of Oaklanders chose to repurpose their building so it could become a hub for all of the groups, organizations and culture workers who were working to create peace *so that no one would have to bear the burden of confronting violence alone.* As we celebrate our fifth anniversary, we are a collective made up of 40 organizations who served almost 90,000 community members last year.

It has not been easy for us either. Cultural groups not used to sharing space with each other were not able to resolve their conflicts easily. Different philosophies about how to keep people safe meant inconsistencies around when and whether to call the police if there was an incident on site. Some partners engage in the work transactionally and some engage as collaborators, and we don't always know how to create an expectation of equal investment by all partners. During our biggest event ever, disability justice activists let us know that we had no right to call our event the "Together We Can Resource Fair" when we weren't providing accessible bathrooms for people with disabilities in our ancient facility and not creating a scent-free environment for people with severe chemical sensitivities.

And the work of building relationship and listening to people from the margins has resulted in magical things happening at the OPC that I could never have created if I sought to build something by myself. In 2014, we hosted listening sessions with OPC partners to create some shared values in response to racially based conflicts between partners and the question over whether every tenant in the building should be required to adhere to an LGBTQ-inclusive policy. In those conversations, shared values emerged that I could not have anticipated. For example, a young Black activist said he'd like to see water bottle filling stations installed around the building to reflect our environmental values. In response, an indigenous elder suggested that, since it would be years before we'd be rehabbing the building, we might practice our environmental commitments in a different way in the meantime: every time an OPC partner holds an event in our building, the event will begin by acknowledging the sacredness of the land and its original inhabitants, which has created a new default in us as a community. When we do begin to rehab the building, we will do so already saturated with a consciousness of the sacredness of the land and our obligations towards it.

And even the parts that have been hard have encouraged us to grow into who we are as a community. The shared value that took the most conversation was one that originally stated we would call police as a last resort. One of our partners who works with youth said we needed to make it "never call the police." A restorative justice partner said there were good alternatives we could utilize and create procedures around. A network called POOR Magazine pointed out that homeless people and people with disabilities and non-English speakers stood a significant risk of being harmed by police specifically in those last-resort moments (as do people of color and youth) and they offered to provide training for us so we could develop a different strategy to create a safe community for all of our partners, clients, neighbors and community as a whole. (We just had it, and dozens of young white hipsters from the neighborhood also attended so they can learn how to play a role in reducing police brutality by not being the ones to invite police into situations others are better equipped to handle.)

Those moments of disappointment from our friends in the disability justice movement are a reminder that we need to institutionalize our values and not simply rely on good intent. Good intent does not give someone a place to pee; a policy of renting an ADA port-o-potty for every major event until we rehab the bathrooms does. We're seeking to get in front of conflict by including restorative justice circles into our employee handbook as the first strategy for responding to staff conflict, inviting in RJ-trained partners to facilitate.

We're developing an advisory council made of clients of our partners so that the community we build moving forward remains accountable to the people we serve and stand in solidarity with, even when our board is diverse and faithful and not exceptionally privileged. We continue to listen to those on the margins and turn our attention away from the center we believe to be failing everyone around it. We maybe even strive to build a community that will no longer have a center and margins 50 years from now.

Most importantly, and germane to this book although never explicitly stated, we see the foundations of our community and our work in the Swahili phrase "Ubuntu," which loosely translates to "I am because you are" or "I am because we are." We have seen the myth of individualism leave too many people isolated and struggling. (I believe that this myth of individualism is one of the original sins of this nation, creating a lie that isolates us and leaves us either feeling like failures when we can't achieve perfection on our own or making us believe that our successes are all our own instead of the result of a community carrying us.) As hard as constantly deepening our relationships can be, we know it is essential for us to building a community that provides for all people's needs while nurturing all people's gifts. It is not the only way to survive, but the principle of Ubuntu is the only way to thrive. And so we practice living into the power of being who we've been taught to be, the power of all of our ancestors only erased in the last several hundred years and replaced with a myth that independence is possible, the lie that interdependence is weak, and the troubling secret that isolation is killing our individual spirits as well as our collective spirit.

I mention all of this for one reason. In this historic moment in the United States, there are a lot of national decisions that are having very clear impacts on local communities. Local schools, churches and synagogues are wondering whether they should become "sanctuary congregations" that harbor refugees whom the government wants to send back to places where they will be killed. Farming communities are wondering how to sustain their economy if immigrant workers are deported when local residents won't work on the farms. People with disabilities and preexisting health issues worry that they may lose healthcare coverage if they change jobs and insurers. LGBTQ people are worried about proposed legislation that correlates with an increase in violence directed towards their communities. And these issues happen alongside continuing issues such as rust belt towns facing low employment and low pay for labor, and Black and Brown communities continuing to face disproportionate rates of incarceration and very limited options for people returning to their communities after extended stays in prison. And on top of that, people of all colors and races face the daily grind of earning enough to support families and having any time left over to enjoy their friends, families, faith communities and hobbies.

We are not in the days of Franco's Spain or Vichy France, but we are now in times when, to paraphrase Pastor Trocmé, our individual and community efforts to do small acts of resistance and hope and accountability either with or as people on the margins are necessary.

And those actions were always necessary. Which is why this book could be twice as thick with twice as many illustrations of everyday heroes and sheroes in our midst using practical steps to get at healing and transformation of their communities.

Those actions are not only necessary; they are eminently achievable. Having a PhD in economics or being a seasoned community organizer, political operative or a fundraising guru can be incredibly helpful at a certain point in the process of neighborhood transformation. But we don't need all of that at the very beginning. We are, it turns out, enough. The people in this book are exceptional. They are smart. They are gifted.

Those skills, though, aren't why they ended up in this book. They ended up in this book because they cared, and because they collaborated. And that continues to transform their communities.

I genuinely hope that the tools and models in this book prove useful to you. I have witnessed the power of asset-based community development and restorative justice and truth commissions and World Café and spiritual grounding of social change work. I have seen the harm that comes from their opposites. I believe that in combination, these processes can take a vision and move it towards reality, when ego is checked at the door so communities can create solutions shaped by many voices, not just the voices of the powerful.

But what matters to me most in writing this book is the following:

You are exceptional. You are smart. You are gifted.

If you care and seek to collaborate, you will transform your community.

And we do not have time for you to feel prepared and worthy. We need you to join with others to heal your neighborhood now. Do it as a beacon of hope or as a sign of resistance or simply as a way of living out who you know you are. Do it for your neighborhood, and do it so that others who feel unprepared and unworthy know that is not an impossible barrier for them.

The cult of individualism has damaged our communities for too long. It is time for us to accept our power to heal our neighborhoods, together. The Arizmendi in me thanks the Arizmendi in you.